THE LIVING AND THE DEAD

Moira Geoghegan

authorHOUSE®

AuthorHouse™ UK Ltd.
500 Avebury Boulevard
Central Milton Keynes, MK9 2BE
www.authorhouse.co.uk
Phone: 08001974150

© 2009 Moira Geoghegan. All rights reserved.

No part of this book may be reproduced, stored in a retrieval system, or transmitted by any means without the written permission of the author.

First published by AuthorHouse 12/23/2009

ISBN: 978-1-4490-0662-4 (sc)

This book is printed on acid-free paper.

This book, like my previous one, is dedicated to my family, both here on earth and in the Spirit World

Acknowledgements:

I would like to acknowledge and thank the following people: My daughter Tina Boydell, for designing the cover of this book and helping me acquire photographs; my cousin Kathleen Purcell of Graiguenamanagh, for photographs of my grandmother and great-grandmother; my other cousin, Chris Kelly, who also supplied pictures; and of course my family who have supported me down through the years and helped me in so many ways.

Thanks to the *Kilkenny People*, *Kilkenny Voice*, *Kilkenny Advertiser* newspapers and freelance journalist John Fitzgerald for highlighting my work and promoting awareness of this and my previous book.

Thanks to the helpful and accommodating staff at *Hot Shotz* Digital Photography Studio of Kieran Street, Kilkenny, for their top-notch professionalism, efficiency, and excellent service, and to Aidan O' Dwyer at the *Kapelli Hair Salon* in Bennettsbridge, for a service that I heartily recommend.

Thanks also to the enormously talented Liana Lovie, the psychic/spiritual artist based in Fethard, County Tipperary, who painted the picture of one of my very helpful spiritual guides. Liana makes the hidden world visible through her beautiful work.

Worthy of mention too is *Ait an Turas*, described as a "place of pilgrimage" located on Achill Island, County Mayo, where spiritual/alternative healing occurs and a wide range of courses and workshops are held for anyone wishing to learn more about the psychic side of life.

Most importantly of all, I pay tribute to my loved ones in the Spirit World and to all my friends on the earth plane; and of course a special thanks to **all** the good people who have called to me for readings over the years. This book honours them.

☙

I include the following letter at the request of Andrea Bonny, a very brave young Dublin girl who had to cope with the death of her twin sister Shelly.

Andrea's moving poetry features in the pages of this book, as a tribute to her own courage and talent and also as a reminder of the glorious truth that, no matter how we lose our loved ones, *we'll meet them again…*

A Tribute to Moira Geoghegan...
by Andrea Bonny

I wrote this letter when my twin sister died, in May 2005. I have kept this letter with Michelle's personal belongings, and kept it to myself until now. Ever since reading Moira's Geoghegan's book Loved Ones, I'm Only a Whisper Away; I wanted to meet her in person.

I went to see her in August of this year.

My Mam was very emotional after seeing Moira, knowing Moira told her Michelle was a very special angel.

I got to speak to Moira for a few moments and was very taken aback at everything she told me. It was amazing. She answered everything I wanted to know about in the letter I had written to Michelle.

I got messages, love, and a laugh from Michelle through Moira.

If you have lost a loved one as I have done, do not question or torment yourself as to where they are.

They are truly gone to the Spirit World in Heaven, and we

WILL meet them again when it is our time.

I have been promised this.

Andrea.

Introduction

Four years have passed since I launched my first book, *Loved Ones, I'm only a whisper Away*. It is still selling, and seldom does a week go by without someone reacting to it.

From all over Ireland, letters continue to arrive at my home, from people who wish to let me know that they have derived benefit either from the book itself or from a psychic reading with me.

The weight of correspondence grows by the day, increasing in volume as I receive warm plaudits and commendations, each of which I read with gratitude and humility, grateful that I can bring healing where there is pain, peace where there is discord, and the joy of knowing there *really is an afterlife*…to replace the fear of death and despair of living that ignorance and materialism has spawned in a world that has to a large extent lost touch with the Greater Reality.

It would take a dedicated band of postal officials to sift through all the letters of support and solidarity I have received over the years!

I am heartened by the extent to which my previous book has helped people, not just in terms of learning more about the Spirit World and life's true purpose…but also in coping with the day-to-day struggles and challenges of life.

A common refrain in the seemingly endless chorus of thanksgiving has been: *"the book helped us to better understand the problems we face and how to resolve these in a way that brings healing rather than discord"*.

That message, expressed in varying tones, accents, and phrasing, has been delivered to me loud and clear and I am delighted by the continuing positive feedback to a book that I hoped would enable me to share my own knowledge and experience of all things psychic with a wider public.

But readers also conveyed a second, equally strong message to me. They were anxious to delve *further* into the mysteries of life, death, and the afterlife.

So I decided, after much soul-searching and due consideration of the issues involved, to publish a second book.

In this, I wish to build on the foundations laid in my first publication. I again adopt a twin-pronged approach to this vast and multi-faceted subject…dealing with both the spiritual and psychic aspects that people find so engrossing, and the more mundane social and practical earthly issues that affect all of us as we progress, sometimes smoothly and sometimes painfully, along the pathways of life.

Thus, you will find yourself reading, in one chapter, about spirit guides or the psychic significance of dreams…and in another about spousal abuse, bullying, or how *not* to prolong a relationship that is past and gone.

Different, widely varying issues…but all strictly relevant to the soul's marathon journey on the earth plane…and the spiritual forces that shape our destiny.

You will appreciate that, as a medium, I feel passionately about the great and glorious **TRUTH** that is survival of death.

Whilst people are free to argue the pros and cons of life after death, to make statements and pen articles or theses for or against…to speculate endlessly on the subject, my position is made quite definite and uncompromising by virtue of the fact that *I know* that death is but a milestone along the path of spiritual evolution and growth.

We are as much alive a minute or an hour or a day or a week after our discarded physical bodies are buried or cremated as we were **before** the sad funeral event and the "final" farewells.

More alive…because our awareness is greatly enhanced when our consciousness transfers to the spirit body…all the old discomforts and restrictions, accumulated over a lifetime long or short, are cast off like a heavy old coat that we no longer need.

We are lighter after the transition, free as the wind, and ready for the next phase of our development as spiritual beings.

That is why I have decided upon a coloured coffin, possibly bright pink, to contain my own mortal remains when my time comes to exit the earth permanently and transfer to the glories of the Spirit World. I prefer an optimistic celebratory colour because the occasion will, for me, be a joyous one.

A bright and breezy design on a grave stone memorial can appeal to a medium. He or she is aware that death is not the awful calamity it appears to be in the context of a mindset enmeshed in materialism and unbelief. Hence we see it from a totally different perspective.

Those of us who are privileged to know the truth about the afterlife from firsthand knowledge have every reason not to fear death, and indeed the best of reasons to look forward to that inevitable departure from a world of pain, trials, and hardship.

Thus it was that the great spiritual masters and initiates of the ancient world *welcomed* death with a smile…instead of shrinking from it in dread and trepidation.

As the big moment approached, they prepared themselves emotionally, physically, and psychologically for the wonderful new life awaiting them.

They surrendered themselves to the natural process that is the disintegration of the mortal body and liberation of their spirits from the constrictions and trappings of flesh and blood forms that they realised were no longer necessary once they ascended into the higher world.

Modern day notions of freezing corpses in the hope that these might be revived at some future date when science has devised more medical cures for illness and disease are pointless.

Such a concept ignores and overlooks the reality that ALL of us survive death…and that the physical body we leave behind is but a shell once we have vacated it. Even if the discarded corpse could be revived, the original occupant would long since have departed the earth plane and be happily engaged in his or her life in the spirit realm.

Science fails to grasp or comprehend that the mortal body is but a temporary vessel of the spirit, that once we have completed our allotted span on earth, *we no longer need* it…that death is simply a casting off…a shedding…of something we no longer need when we progress to the next level of consciousness and state of being.

So while others debate…and wonder…we mediums say to you: hey, it's okay…the Spirit World is real…and nobody is ever lost. All your loved ones are safe and well over there and you will join them in good time.

I want all readers of this book to replace any fear of death they might hold…with courage…*and the certainty that they will walk away intact from the Big D.*

Life after death is not a mere conceptual or abstract theory or a nifty idea, or just a consoling or tactful notion to assuage grief. It is a solid *fact*, and a cause to celebrate life.

There is, I hope, something for everybody in the pages that follow. But the one essential message I want readers to take away with them is this:

Do what you know is right in life and respect the rights and feelings of your fellow human beings.

Do this…and great will be your reward in the afterlife!

1

Bridging the Gulf between Two Worlds

As I mentioned in my previous book, I was aware from an early age that people around me couldn't see what I saw, nor hear what I heard. I therefore had to learn to be careful and to show tact in all my routine day-to day social dealings.

I had to control my psychic ability, and hold back from revealing the wonderful truth that was so evident to me and yet, I knew, hidden from so many of my fellow humans. There were times when my family cautioned: Don't mention that! Say nothing about spiritual beings!

I never held that against my family, or indeed anyone else either because I understood their fear of the unknown. They were nervous. They didn't understand the abilities I had, or whence I had received these treasured gifts.

From my twenties onwards, I was working closely with the Spirit World to convey the magnificent and reassuring certainty of life after death to anyone prepared to listen.

I had long come to accept that the voices I heard or perceived telepathically were real, that they were those of people who once lived and worked and loved and laughed here on earth. This was, of course, an enormously significant realisation on my part.

The implications of knowing that life continues after so-called death are so far-reaching! This knowledge gives you a whole new perspective on your present earthly life. You can relax and stop worrying about the prospect of death being the end, or a grim snuffing out of the flickering flame of existence.

You know, when you are a medium, that dying to the earth world is akin to casually throwing open a door of the room you are in and entering the next room…of closing that door on the shadowy, strife-laden, sorrow-filled, pain-racked space you have occupied for your allotted earthly life-span and opening the door that leads into a haven of light, peace, love, and tranquillity.

This is not a mere fanciful notion, or a series of words designed purely to console. It is the plain, unadulterated truth. Religions and belief systems of all shades that differ in a thousand ways agree on that one central point that I emphasise from my own personal knowledge: That when you draw or exhale your last breath on this earth you begin a new life *elsewhere*.

The difference between religious faith or belief and my own position as a medium is that I know from personal first-hand experience that the afterlife is a fact…I don't have to rely on supposition or "wishful thinking" or any kind of faith.

This is why I can speak with absolute authority and a sincere heart to those who come to me for readings.

I can assure them without the slightest scintilla of doubt or wavering that their loved ones that they mourn… are in the Spirit World, and that they will see them again when they too cross over at a later stage.

Sharing the Pain…

With the gift comes a curious price I have to pay for the rare privilege that is mine. When people come to me for readings I don't just listen to their troubles and empathise with the manifold challenges that assail human beings.

I literally *feel* the pain of the ones who have passed over and communicate with my clients. I mean of course the suffering they endured *on earth*, because once they make the transition to the Spirit World all pain ceases.

When a spirit tells me how he or she died, I may experience for a moment or two a sensation recalling the nature of the illness or accident or violent event that caused physical death. I *connect* with their past pain and suffering momentarily so that I can honestly tell the client sitting there in the consultation room how the loved one passed over.

I can feel the fear that may have accompanied the dying process, the anxiety, and the panic born of misunderstanding death. Sometimes, when a spirit comes through at a reading who died of cancer and had a lot of intensive medical treatment in the weeks and months leading up to death, I feel physically sick and nauseous for a few seconds.

I experience a spirit person's earthly heart attack quite intensely. I feel as though my chest were expanding and about to explode.

If the spirit crossed over by suicide, I can feel the tightening of a rope (in the case of hanging), or the sensation of desperation preceding the act of self-killing. Whatever the cause of a spirit's transition, I will pick it up.

A drowning translates for me as a difficulty to breathe or swallow… with pneumonia a tightening of the chest and lungs.

People commit suicide usually when very deeply depressed and see no way out of their earthly situations. They may have second thoughts when they hit the water, or once the noose begins to tighten, or the drug takes effect. Then it is too late.

So yes, in addition to the inestimable rewards that flow from mediumship, there is a daily cross to carry. I have carried that cross for decades. I have to quietly heave it up unto my back whenever I facilitate the trans-dimensional contact that is helpful and reassuring to bereaved people who yearn for evidence that they will meet their loved ones again.

It can be an exhaustive and draining experience…taking on the pain of others and sharing their sorrow. Very often, the person sitting there in front of me doesn't realise this, and is unaware of the energies at work in the communication process. They see a medium at work, and await the messages, but don't always understand what is happening.

In passing, I might mention that I have never yet met another medium that has been blessed with quite the same range of abilities, and especially this ability to take on some of the suffering that accompanies the dying process.

In meditation, I have to ask the Higher Spirit to take away some of the pain and heartache that I accumulate during readings.

The sharing of pain that I experience is rare even among the practising mediums of this world. A medium named Adele Maginot is recalled by psychic researchers as having felt a strong, almost overpowering sensation of choking while in trance as she described how a spirit communicator had passed over by that cause of death.

Another medium, not Irish or based in this country, said she had an intense pain in her abdomen accompanied by thirst when facilitating a spirit communicator who had died of liver cancer.

I experience pain of a different kind when some happily married people call for readings and I am shown how the romances or marriages will flounder down the line, leading to second and maybe third marriages for them.

Though the merry sound of wedding bells may still be ringing inside their bliss-filled heads, I can sense the storm clouds of dissolving relationships brewing on the far horizons… I can sense the approaching unhappy scenario.

I have to be tactful when I perceive such "trouble ahead", not only because I don't wish to upset the client, but because in the last analysis people have to learn from their mistakes and acquire a deeper appreciation of the true meaning of life by their own decisions and actions, freely taken and carried through.

I can only guide, point the way. But I cannot force anyone to change his or her life-style. People have to change from within, to learn their lessons in the great School of Life into which they were born willingly and with the intention to learn and evolve and become spiritually better people.

Unfortunately the good intentions we have prior to leaving the Spirit World to experience yet another earth incarnation are all too easily forgotten or put aside as we traverse the road of life and become sidetracked by all the false values and temptations that litter the metaphorical "Highway to Heaven".

We have to take stock every now and then and focus on the true values that will count when our turn comes to return to the Spirit World.

If we cheat on our husbands or wives, or engage in any evil acts that cause malicious harm or hurt or injury to others, we hold back our progress in the afterlife.

Instead of rising to the higher planes of that "Far Country" beyond earth, we will have to linger in the lower vibratory levels until we see sense and purge ourselves of such ill-intent, malice, cruelty, or downright nastiness.

One of the hardest parts of mediumship is when I perceive that a young person who has called for a reading hasn't got a long earth life ahead of him or her. I can't mention what I see in that instance, or at least not directly. It would be unethical to frighten the sitter or press any panic buttons.

I know what awaits them, and have to accept they are likely to keep their appointments with destiny. Though seemingly tragic, the untimely departure of these young souls from life on earth will, as with all deaths, usher them into the light and happiness of the Spirit World where loved ones wait to receive them.

Of course the pain and heartache that I perceive in the earthly lives of people who have passed is more than offset by the sheer joy and relief I also experience in readings.

I get to meet the kindest and loveliest of people in my work, both in spirit and earthly human form. On both sides of the "veil" I encounter the hopes, dreams, simple delights, and fond memories that make life worth living for the majority of people, whatever challenges they have to address along the way.

I glimpse the pure, unconditional love that pours forth from spirit to loved ones who are still fulfilling their life-missions, slogging it out and striving as best they can to achieve their God-given potential as human beings.

I share in the humbling and ennobling milestones that mark those special junctures along life's obstacle-strewn highway…the joy of a birthday…a wedding anniversary…first or last day at school…the first kiss…all the small and not so small occasions that remain illuminated in human memory even when millions of other moments or events have faded from our minds.

The spirits show me those happy times; recreate them for me. Being clairaudient, they are audible to me so I am privileged to hear their voices, and as a clairvoyant I can perceive with enhanced sight the glorious abode of spirit that awaits us all when we too make that transition to our true home.

So yes, the pain is swept away by the joy of knowing that a better world follows this one of sorrow. I contrast the suffering caused by cancer, heart ailments, accidental death, and the thousands of other ailments by which we take our leave of earth-life…with what comes after.

Though privileged to know this great truth, I am also profoundly conscious of the immense responsibility that goes with it. To facilitate communication between this and another dimension with a view to giving people "word" of their loved ones is an enormous breakthrough for anyone who, up to that point, disbelieved in an afterlife or feared they would never again see those precious friends or family members.

I take that responsibility seriously. I am a messenger of spirit, a bringer of tidings from the world beyond and the bearer of the best news of all for anyone assailed by doubts about human survival of death: You'll be fine!

Let me share with you an insight that came to me in meditation: ***"God said I will give you spirit and you will know that life is nothing but circles…a continuous circle without end. It is eternal. The body I give you does not belong to you. It belongs to me. The body I give belongs to Mother Earth and shall return to the Earth Mother when earth life ends."***

As a medium I accept the implications of my life-mission and I honour the voice of my Creator within me.

But of course…no matter how often people are assured of survival beyond death, doubt lingers…scepticism gnaws at the heart, tormenting with its grim prompting of uncertainty and the half-promise of nothingness after life on earth.

Do not waste a single moment worrying about human mortality. The notion of human extinction at the point of death is the ultimate illusion and cry of despair. But, and I cannot emphasise this strongly enough or often enough: It is a *needless* worry…because the reality of the afterlife is as palpable and obvious and evident to a medium like myself as the everyday world of atoms and solid objects and people walking up and down streets.

As one who can see and hear the Spirit World…the ineffable beauty and breathtaking loveliness of it, I say to you: **<u>Stop Worrying!</u>**

When you see, as I have seen, the crippled walk again, the dumb happily converse again, the paralysed once again brimming with life and vitality, the blind beholding the wonders of the universe with spirit sight, the deaf hearing with the greatest clarity on the Other Side… when you see little children who have died to the earth plane restored to health and happiness in the Spirit World…then you will realise how "off the beaten track" the gloomy atheists and materialistic Nay-Sayers have been in their attacks on your belief in the afterlife!

Coping with Bereavement

You can shed tears that he is gone…
Or you can smile because he has lived.

You can close your eyes and pray that he'll come back,
Or you can open your eyes and see all that he has left.

Your heart can be empty because you can't see him
Or you can be full of the love you shared.

You can turn your back on tomorrow and live yesterday,
Or you can be happy for tomorrow because of yesterday.

You can remember him and only that he's gone,
Or you can cherish his memory and let it live on.

You can cry and close your mind, be empty and turn back…
Or you can do what he'd want:
Smile…open your eyes…love…
And Live on.

2

Easement the Pain of Bereavement…

Being able to see life from both sides…from the angle of the earth plane AND the Spirit World has of course given me a different perspective on human existence and on all aspects of life than that of most non-psychic men and women.

It is because I am aware of what awaits us after death, and of the **TRUE PURPOSE** of life on earth, that I seek to alert all of you to this reality.

I wish to ensure that as many of you as possible will avoid taking that disastrous wrong turning along life's highway that will hold up your progress as spiritual beings that, for the moment, occupy physical bodies but some day will depart the earth plane to commence the next stage of existence in the Spirit World.

In the readings I arrange for the many people who call to me, I witness day in and day out…the appalling consequences of humanity's *dark side*.

Equally, I am privileged to experience those moments of joy and celebration, those tears of relief that flow when a loved one that a caller feared was lost or gone forever …suddenly comes through with a reassuring message…a calling card of love and heartening support from across time and space…to let that person sitting there in front of me in the consultation room know there is, to quote Shakespeare, *a world elsewhere.*

I will never forget the day a woman called in who had lost three sons to the tragedy of suicide. I saw them in their spiritual forms, anxious to embrace her with love. They desperately wanted her to know that they were at peace, that despite the horrific mode of their passing, they were now free from pain and receiving healing in their new world.

She pleaded with them, asking them why they didn't seek help for whatever drove them to end their earth lives. She would have been there for them if they had sought help or support, she told them. And all the usual regrets and "what ifs" that follow a suicide escaped her lips. It was a deeply emotional scene.

Her sons assured her, through me, that they had come to terms with the issues and motivations that had led to their decision to quit life on earth before their time.

I deal with suicide in chapter ten, and I repeat what I have said in that chapter and in my previous book. **If you feel suicidal, seek immediate help**.

If you know, or suspect, that someone is contemplating suicide, don't be afraid to intervene. Suicide is NEVER a solution but ALWAYS a tragedy.

It inflicts untold suffering on those left behind and it is of *no spiritual benefit whatsoever* to you to commit suicide. You are holding up your spiritual progress by taking this exit from the physical plane…and behind you, back on earth, you are leaving a legacy of indescribable sorrow and bereavement.

I remember another woman who wanted to know if her husband, now in the Spirit world, was still the same contrary and cantankerous fellow he had been on earth. I noticed this lady had lines of sorrow and hardship clearly etched in her face, and that she looked far older than her age. This was due to a difficult life.

He came through at the reading, expressing regret at not having treated her better, and taking her for granted. He was crying, I had to tell the woman, and he really was filled with remorse.

But she was having none of it. She insisted she had no intention of "spending eternity" with him, after all those years of his nasty mood swings and selfish behaviour. All he had ever brought her was pain and anxiety.

He apologised, as spirits so often do in these situations. But she was adamant. He had his chance and he had blown it. She wouldn't be re-uniting with him on the Other Side.

But as the reading progressed, and I passed on further messages from her husband, she mellowed somewhat.

Her bitterness abated and gave way to a softer tone and attitude. She showed signs of healing, of coming to terms with the fact that nobody is perfect and that her husband just *might* be entitled to forgiveness.

She relented in her hostility towards him, and he, for his part, had accepted responsibility for his failure to fulfil his side of the "love honour and cherish" pledge they both had made on their wedding day. By the time she was ready to leave my consultation room; this woman was more at peace with herself…and her husband.

This is just one example of how mediumship can make such a huge, life-changing difference to people…both here on earth and in the Spirit World.

It opens channels of communication that enable disputes to be detoxified or rendered less bitter…if not always to be resolved. There needs to far more of this trans-dimensional contact between our world and the one beyond.

It is, in essence, the ultimate form of healing!

You will see your Child Again!

Since I wrote about the pain and heartache of children passing over in my first book, many people have shared their own feelings and experience of this bitter milestone in their lives. They cannot understand why a child should die before the parents.

Most parents naturally expect that their children will outlive them by many years. They expect them to be around in the autumn or winter of their own lives to comfort them and maybe even to look after them to some extent.

Having brought a child into the world, the parents treasure the precious baby and take pride in each stage of the child's growth and development…the first sounds that are almost words…the first tentative steps as he or she learns to walk. The child is more precious than silver or gold to caring parents.

How devastating then is the death of a child. It is, for most parents, their worst nightmare, something they cannot accept or ever come to terms with, to have their baby or toddler or teenage son or daughter cruelly snatched from them, shattering all their fond hopes and dreams for the beloved one.

From the moment the child leaves them, the parents embark on a long grief-stricken journey that seemingly has no end. Friends and neighbours console them, but often to no avail. It seems the grieving and the sorrow will go on forever. Years pass, and yet the pain of separation remains; the perennial aching of the heart for one beloved and now elsewhere.

As a medium, I want to again reassure everyone reading this who may be affected by such a tragedy that the child whose death you mourn is **not** lost to you forever. What you see at the sad day of mourning in a church or cemetery does not represent the final chapter in your child's innocent life.

Earthly appearances are so deceptive. Let me tell you what I see…

not the sad white coffin being lowered into the ground or conveyed in a hearse. Those are just the trappings of earthly ritual, man-made religious customs and ceremonies.

I see the child fully alive in spirit, full of life and vitality and eager to let you know that all is well, that they've passed to a different, kinder world where you will someday be re-united with them.

At readings, I have had bereaved parents of children who passed over seeking advice and understanding. As they share their grief, the child of whom they speak may communicate, mainly through a spirit guide acting on his or her behalf.

Reader! If only you could see, hear, and sense what I do on these occasions: The spirit children saying: "tell mammy I'm here", maybe showing them dolls or other toys, trying to make their presence known to the grieving parent sitting there in the room.

It is a deeply moving, humbling experience, for me as well for as the parent. I describe what is happening, and relay any messages received to the parent. I tell them of the beautiful scenes in the Spirit World that accompany the passing over of a child.

I explain that no child is lost, that each and every one is cared for in a loving environment on the Other Side. These children grow to maturity and receive a full education in the world beyond this one.

Andrea Bonny of Dublin wrote the following lovely letter…to her twin sister Shelly, who had crossed to the Spirit World. I am delighted to include it with this chapter. Andrea speaks for so many people, of all cultures and nations, and of all ages, when she expresses her feelings for her sister and the hope that they'll meet again:

A Letter from the Heart...
From Andrea to her dear sister
Shelly

Dear Shelly,

I used to ask myself... if there were really was a place out there where loved ones who passed away have gone.

I wondered if I will ever meet them again one day, like you hear about in films and stories.

People make it out to be so beautiful, and peaceful, beyond your wildest dreams...but is this real?

Nobody understands how I'm feeling since you've gone... Shelly...I try to talk to people, but I can't tell them exactly how I feel. It's hard.

I get so angry and cannot control it...as much as I try. But nobody knows how it feels to lose your twin.

I don't understand why you had to go and why God could take such a good person. I know you're an angel in Heaven now... God is taking good care of you for me.

I just wish I could take you back for a day... or even just an hour... so I could give you one last hug. I can't believe you're gone.

It's like a bad dream and I haven't woken up yet. I miss you so much. I feel scared, even though you're with me every day. I feel like I'm always alone with you.

School is hard. We were meant to start secondary school together. We even got our uniforms fitted together, and did our entrance test together.

Shortly after we made our Confirmation, you were gone. It was heartbreaking. I often got upset in school, thinking of you. I found it hard to concentrate and get things done.

You should be here with me, Shelly. It's not fair.

I'm afraid of doing things and going places by myself, because we were always together, and I miss that.

I know we used to fight over the most ridiculous things…like cleaning our rooms or clothes!

I miss even those fights.

I try to think of the good memories we had…and find me laughing to myself. We had the best times together.

Without even trying you were funny, you would make people laugh. You always put a smile on everybody's face.

You were the best sister and friend anyone could have.

You will always be my best friend. I miss you so much Michelle.

I'm always thinking of you.

Love you always,

Andrea xxx

3

Trance and Séance

Trance

People ask: what is trance and what happens to a medium who enters this state of consciousness?

In trance, a medium partly or completely loses consciousness and as a rule will not be aware of what transpires during the reading. In this state, the medium's body may be temporarily taken over or controlled by a spiritual entity who then may speak using the vocal chords of the medium.

A Control is sometimes referred to in spiritualist literature as a kind of "Master of Ceremonies", a spirit who acts as a helpful intermediary between the medium and the various spirits that wish to communicate.

The Control helps to strengthen the communication process and enhance the clarity of the messages being delivered from the Spirit World to the incarnate person who has approached the medium for a reading.

Most mediums have Spirit Guides who protect them during this complex process, to ensure that no malevolent entities can invade or interfere with their minds or bodies. I have my Guides, who have served me well for years.

I include in this book a painting by a talented clairvoyant artist of one of my guides. Like so many other great spirits, he is busily helping humanity on its upward spiral of evolutionary growth, in his case specialising in the art and science of healing.

What kinds of message are received in trances?

Just about every kind, ranging from seemingly trivial or amusing ones to profoundly thought-provoking messages.

For some people, the best messages are evidential…offering proof that their loved ones have survived death and arrived safely on the Other Side.

This is accomplished by reference to facts or memories or circumstances that only the sitter and the communicating spirit could have known about. The sitter will then be assured that the message is coming from the loved one.

Séance

This is where a group of people assemble to make contact with the Spirit World, one of whom should ideally be an experienced medium. Those present may form a circle and join hands, before one of them is ready to pose questions or seek out any spiritual presence in the room, which is usually darkened.

At the turn of the 20th century séances were quite popular in Britain and America, with sittings taking place in many households in an attempt to communicate with other dimensions.

A drawback in this type of attempted communication with the Spirit World is that dark or mischievous entities may interfere with the process, or even succeed in attacking the participants, so it is essential in any séance involving a group of non-psychics that a capable medium is present to ensure that the circle is protected from the negative forces, for, as asserted elsewhere in this book, evil influences are never too far away and if the opportunity arises, they will manifest, possibly with far-reaching unhealthy implications for anyone targeted by them.

To be successful, a group séance traditionally depended on an equal number of male and female participants.

Ideally, each person sitting around the table should be open-minded about the procedure and not overtly hostile to the planned attempt at trans-dimensional communication.

Sceptics can be a serious drawback at a séance, as can people who have any serious troubles on their minds that serve to distract their thoughts from the matter in hand.

As a rule, the group will utilise a round table rather than a square or rectangular one, to facilitate a circular formation.

Once seated and ready to get the proceedings underway, the sitters will place their hands on the table, fingers touching the hands next to them, or maybe, if preferred clasping these.

The person who is acting as medium, who ideally is a trained or experienced one, will then commence his or her efforts to open the channels of communication with the Spirit World.

Throughout the séance, the other sitters should be careful not to disturb or distract or physically grab the medium during trance, as this can cause a severe shock or extreme discomfort.

In the old days, people liked to precede the séance with a hymn or a prayer, or the playing of soft music, in order to create a harmonious atmosphere in the room. It is deemed advisable to use a room that is sparsely furnished and does not have any ostentatious or overly eye-catching wall hangings or other objects that might distract sitters.

The avoidance of bright lights during the séance is important too, as this can distract the medium. One should also, if possible, check that the room is wind and breeze-proof and that no tricks or fraud of any kind can be perpetrated, as this completely defeats the purpose of the exercise.

If physical, as distinct from mental, mediumship, is involved, the spiritual presence in the room may be heralded by a gentle gust of cold or cool air, felt by one or more of the sitters. Rapping noises may also be heard, and lights seen to appear at various points in the room.

A mental medium, that is one who receives the spirit communication via his or her mind rather than through physical sounds and sights, will instead simply declare that spiritual contact has occurred or is occurring.

In the days physical mediumship was widely practised, you might see the table rise off the ground during a séance, or the medium herself. Apports were common. These are solid objects that materialise literally out of thin air at the séance and can be retained by whomsoever the spirit hands them too, or whoever happens to pick them up when they appear.

Ghostly music or voices were also a common feature of physical mediumship séances.

While this kind of mediumship has served to provide further evidence to sceptics that the afterlife is real, I would point out that mental mediums are equally persuasive in the way we channel spirits and facilitate trans-dimensional contact.

There is no need for dramatic manifestations to reassure people that their loved ones are safe and well in the Spirit World. Such assurances can be transmitted calmly and quietly, and in a relaxed environment as I have done in my own work.

I find that I can relay those messages of hope and love from the world beyond without recourse to any procedure that would *frighten* a client or make them feel uncomfortable.

Your loved ones want you to know they are happy and at peace, and would not wish you to be frightened or intimidated by any aspect of the spirit communication process. I have always endeavoured to put people at their ease when they arrive for readings.

My priority is to ensure that each person who comes to me will leave **reassured and content**, and not alarmed or discommoded by what is after all a natural and wholesome procedure: letting you know that your friends and family on the Other Side are as alive as you are… though in a different world.

Whether you opt to avail of mental or physical mediumship, remember that it is no more to be feared than dialling a telephone number to speak to a friend here on earth, or answering your phone to hear the voice of a loved one. The only difference is that, if you are not a medium yourself, you need the "operator" to establish contact.

The medium is akin to a telephone operator who acts as a go-between for you and your friend or family member in the Spirit World.

Though all of you may of course speak to your loved ones ANYTIME, just by thinking of them (*your* thoughts can reach the Spirit World too), think of the medium as someone who can "get you a better line" of communication and is more attuned to the higher vibrations of those dimensions that are as real as this material world but invisible to the naked human eye and inaudible to the average human ear in the same way that auras are invisible to most people and certain sounds can be heard by animals but not by humans.

Think of different wavelengths: When you tune into one, you cannot hear the programme on the others…yet the radio waves picked up by those are as real and substantial as the ones creating the sounds on the one you have tuned into.

Because you cannot for the time being perceive a sight or sound or situation doesn't mean it isn't real…only that you have not yet attuned yourself to perceive it.

Don't worry if you are not psychic and cannot see auras, sense spiritual presences, or predict the future…in time you will learn the truth of what I say, when your turn comes to cross the Great Divide.

In the meantime, why not do some research of your own to appraise yourself of the overwhelming evidence that is out there… **confirming that we do indeed survive that much feared and vastly misunderstood event we call death.**

Spirit Photography

Yet another way in which spirits may make their presence known is via photography. Almost everyone has taken a photo at some point in which strange or unfamiliar forms appear that shouldn't be there, or that didn't seem to the photographer to be present when the picture was snapped.

While many such photographs can be explained in terms of defects in the camera or deceptive patterns caused by shadows, panel grains, or outright mischief making on the part of the photographer, a substantial number of pictures do show images that cannot be explained away as tricks of the light or mistaken identification.

In my own career as a psychic and a medium, I have encountered quite a few spirit photographs; that is, pictures that contain images of discarnate entities or energies emanating from the Spirit World.

Pictures taken in my own home show such otherworldly forms and images. But perhaps the most significant ones are those snapped in graveyards, haunted houses, and other locations associated with a concentration of spirit activity.

There was a widely- publicised case a few years ago in which a family in County Kerry circulated a photograph one of them had taken at the funeral of an elderly woman, a relative of theirs.

This shows a graveyard scene with a country church in the background… dominating the picture is a ghostly white image that the family and others who viewed the picture claimed in statements to the media was the Blessed Virgin.

Following the newspaper articles on this controversy, I was contacted by reporters and asked for my own opinion and analysis.

Having examined the picture carefully and reflected on the context in which it was produced, I knew that the image wasn't in fact that of Blessed Virgin. It was, I thought far more likely, the spirit of the woman whose mortal remains had been laid to rest in that graveyard.

Other pictures I have seen have human shapes and representations, again mainly captured on film at funerals or in cemeteries.

People wonder: how can spirits become manifest on film when the average non-clairvoyant person can't see them and they are to all intents and purposes invisible to human eye-sight?

The answer is simply that the camera has a far greater sensitivity to light than the human eye does. It can therefore, in certain circumstances, record images that are not visible to most human beings.

Add to this the determination of a spirit being to make his or her presence known, whether to loved ones on this side or to people in general, and you have the best of reasons for finding such pictorial evidence of that being's continued existence on celluloid.

Scientists, naturally sceptical of anything supporting a belief in the afterlife, dismiss spirit photography in a lot of situations, but even they sometimes have to admit that a photograph *does appear* to be a genuine indicator of otherworldly forces at work.

One such instance was that of the famous Brown Lady of Raynham Hall.

A ghost known as the Brown Lady has apparently haunted an English manor house, in Norfolk, for more than two hundred and fifty years. Her earth life identity has never been formally established, but she is believed to have been Dorothy Townsend, the wife of a powerful titled gentleman.

When her husband found that Dorothy was also another man's mistress, and cheating on him, he cruelly locked her in a room for prolonged periods as punishment. As to her cause of death, there were dark rumours to the effect that somebody pushed her down a stairs.

Up until 1904, a beautiful portrait of Dorothy hung At Raynham Hall. When viewed by day, she seemed happy, with her large eyes radiant and a benign smile on the face.

But at night, witnesses claimed that her facial expression changed by candlelight to one of malice and evil, with the eyes disappearing altogether. Numerous guests staying at the manor house saw her ghost.

Some tried to pursue her along corridors but she just vanished through walls. It was in 1936 that someone had the excellent idea to photograph Lady Dorothy's spirit. The photographer started by taking pictures of a staircase, hoping that perhaps something might show when these were developed.

But as the camera flashed, the photographer and an assistant beheld a sight that left them dumbfounded: A vaporous form began to take shape on the staircase…a woman dressed in white materialised…and she began to step down towards the photographer and others standing at the foot of the staircase.

He summoned up courage to take another picture, this time of the ghostly form descending the staircase.

The picture developed very clearly and confounded many sceptics of the time.

It showed the lady wearing a wedding gown and veil. Scientists and experts of kinds examined the picture but could find no evidence of fraud or camera defects, leading to psychic researchers concluding that it did indeed show the Brown Lady of Raynham Hall.

I reproduce this famous photograph. See what you think of it!

If you want to take spirit photographs, you could start by visiting graveyards or by bringing your camera to funeral parlours. You need to be discreet of course about when you decide to use the camera. You might ask the permission of relatives of the deceased or wait for an opportune moment when the parlour or waking room is empty apart from you, to avoid upsetting anyone.

When you examine the picture afterwards you may, if you are fortunate, find the image or vague semi-transparent silhouette of the person who just said goodbye to this world.

☙

4

How to BEAT the Bullies!

In my previous book, I spoke out against the horrendous practise of workplace bullying. The response my chapter on that issue received prompts me to touch upon it again, as it is surely one of the great social challenges, not only of our present age, but of all times and places.

Over the years, many people have come to me with heart breaking stories of how they were bullied at work. I have listened to accounts of human wickedness and the impact it has had on innocent men and women…whose only crime was to have attracted the attention of bullies.

The harrowing true stories and recollections of this cowardly crime I have heard throughout my career as a medium would draw tears from a stone. Stories of how bullying has wrecked homes and driven people to suicide.

Apart from the legal aspects of this problem, I have to warn anyone who bullies another human being that regardless of how clever or devious they are…they will have to *pay* for that behaviour at a future stage. No action goes unrecorded in the Eternal book of Life.

Think about that…if you contemplate making life hell for another person…you will some day have to account for your actions…and how those actions have altered the lives of others…whether for better or worse.

I know from my work that there is ***no hiding place for bullies in the world beyond this one.*** There is absolute accountability and justice for all.

Let's take a closer look at this dark practise that has been with us for as long as our species first learned to walk upright and found the power of speech on this planet.

Wherever groups of human beings assemble for any purpose, there is the potential for bullying. The workplace, however, is where it can be most lethal because many people are tied financially to their jobs and cannot easily "rock the boat" and risk losing their livelihoods: Hence the tendency for victims of workplace bullying to suffer in silence.

Workplace bullying assumes many forms, all of them detestable and inhuman. It can be verbal... physical... social... or psychological. The bully can be your employer, or manager, foreman (or woman), or one of your fellow workers.

Any work environment can serve as the venue for bullying, whether an office, a factory floor, a building site, a pub...wherever human beings gather to work together at any task or towards any goal.

The most common form of bullying is verbal abuse, directed at the victim, to make fun of him or her, whether on a one to one basis, or in front of other workers.

Or the bully may deliberately offend your family, or make racist or sexist remarks that are intended to hurt, or comments that reflect adversely on your parentage, educational status, or family background.

People have told me of situations where they were "tagged" with the stigma of false allegations, such as that they were sexual perverts... when in fact they were completely innocent of this "tag". Some victims of this kind of gratuitous fabricated stigmatising never recover from the impact of the slur imposed on their innocent reputations.

Mud sticks, and no matter how strenuously they deny the bully's false allegations, they fear that some people will still believe the malicious lies and innuendo.

This is not to be confused with workers having a laugh or sharing a joke together in a fraternal setting. I am thinking here of the hateful use, or misuse, of so-called "humour" that is in obvious bad taste and aimed purely at hurting the feelings and dignity of a fellow worker.

Another bullying approach that can be less conspicuous but equally hurtful, perhaps more so in certain cases, is the tactic of playing cruel mind games on a worker. Some employers and managers resort to this to undermine a worker, especially if they wish him or her to quit the job but have no legitimate grounds on which to ask the person to leave.

So they contrive to isolate or deliberately exclude the targeted individual from activities and social gatherings organised at work or during lunch breaks.

Or they may devise ways of "leaning" on the worker to make life so miserable that he/she just decides to quit.

For example the boss may assign the worker to undertake tasks that are utterly pointless and demeaning, or irrelevant to the job itself; or ones that cannot possibly be completed within the time frame allowed, or he may resort to generally sabotaging your ability to perform your normal daily chores and duties in the workplace.

A subtle form of intimidation favoured by the sophisticated bully in the office environment is to pin those little yellow stickers with curt but unreasonable instructions on an employee's desk when he or she is absent so that the employee is left wondering why the person in charge won't issue these instructions personally.

An unbearable tension and unwarranted anxiety is created over time with this tactic if it continues.

Other employers won't even bother to be so devious. They will just go out of their way to make you feel small and worthless.

This is achieved by hurtful snide references and insinuations, and he may involve one or more of your fellow workers in this twisted scheme. Hurtful remarks with sinister double meanings may form part of the verbal bully's repertoire.

An especially cruel bullying technique is often not recognised for the sick and illegal practise it is: "*Hazing*".

This is where a new recruit or arrival in the workplace is subjected to humiliating and degrading treatment as part of what some workers have decided is an "initiation" for him or her.

The new arrival may be taunted and deliberately shunned or ridiculed until he or she is accepted as a member of the staff or workforce.

This happens in all types of work environment, including teacher staff rooms, hospitals, and newspaper offices. Whatever feeble defences are offered in its favour or excuses made for it, "hazing" is just bullying pure and simple and should be identified as such by anyone who witnesses, or participates, in it.

Physical bullying is more blatant and sometimes, but not always, easier to prove. The bully pushes or roughly nudges the victim in a hostile manner, or in extreme cases punches or kicks or otherwise assaults the person.

Or severe threats of violence may be involved, possibly with a makeshift weapon such as a knife or heavy object brandished to add to the victim's fear of the threat.

Women in particular but men also are subjected to bullying in the form of sexual harassment at work. There may be inappropriate physical contact.

Notoriously, women are sometimes pressurised into sleeping with the boss in order to further their careers. Though they are given the option of not accepting such "offers", they may in certain instances feel obliged to capitulate for the sake of their jobs.

They fear being overlooked for promotion or even losing their jobs if they resist this kind of approach.

The effects of bullying are manifold and potentially devastating. It blows away a person's confidence and self-esteem, replacing these twin pillars of human fulfilment with feelings of fear, anxiety, insomnia, depression, or illness, either mental or physical…or both.

Bullied workers may withdraw from society, lose trust in people generally, and develop an absentee problem that may in turn lead to their being dismissed from their jobs…which in some cases, as already explained, may be exactly what a bullying boss had planned from the first moment he initiated the harassment and intimidation.

People who feel compelled to leave jobs owing to bullying or are dismissed as an indirect result of it often find it difficult to ever trust another employer…or to adjust to a normal work environment again.

In extreme cases, victims may commit suicide. In addition to the indescribable grief and suffering this brings loved ones, I would remind any bullies reading this that **THEY** will bear the responsibility for that person's untimely departure from the earth plane.

Their cruel and wicked acts, their deeply hurtful and soul-destroying behaviour will be deemed to have led to the tragedy.

The bullies themselves have problems too of course. Otherwise they would not engage in this detestable activity that brings untold misery to people's lives.

Some of them suffer from low self-esteem, and because they have little or no respect for themselves they are willing to inflict this injustice on others…to a certain extent it is an expression of self-hatred on their part.

Other bullies may themselves have been bullied and possibly arrived at the conclusion (tragically mistaken) that they too must bully others in order to get by in the world.

They think that by appearing or acting "tough" and making other people suffer they somehow become stronger and more powerful. In fact, the image they project is false and they are just perpetuating the cycle of suffering and misery.

Psychologists have identified different kinds of bullies. One classification concentrates on four especially unpleasant profiles to look out for:

The Screaming Mimi: This fellow humiliates his victims with vicious insults or name-calling in front of other workers in order to establish a tyrannical control over him but also to intimidate any members of the work force who might harbour notions of defying his wishes. This bully poisons the atmosphere in the workplace, generating fear, dampening morale, and undermining the performance of workers.

The Constant Critic or Nitpicker makes false and potentially damaging accusations but he mainly operates *when nobody but his intended victim is around* to witness his actions. He tries to exercise control over his victim by imbuing him or her with a fear of what he can do to them with false allegations. He undermines with persistent, negative and unfair criticism.

The Two-Headed Snake: This unsavoury character is defined as " a duplicitous, passive-aggressive destroyer of reputations through organised rumour-mongering".

The Gatekeeper operates on a different level but is equally destructive in his bullying. He manipulates his victim by withholding resources that the worker needs to accomplish his allotted task or job. He may deny the worker necessary training, time, information, or required permission, thus wrecking his victim's work performance.

Bear in mind too that some bullies prefer to bully by proxy…they use other workers to target their chosen victims, keeping their own hands "clean"…as they see it.

If you are a victim of any type of bullying, you should immediately take steps to face up to and decisively confront the problem.

Remember, you have an absolute human and civil right to work in a safe, healthy, intimidation-free environment and NOBODY has the right to subject you to harassment, threats, violence, or any form of degrading or humiliating treatment.

A word of caution at this point: Let's not confuse bullying with simple arguments and differences of opinion that arise in all work situations, or the conflicts that stem perhaps from personality clashes at work.

If a worker is genuinely out of line because she or he is breaking the rules of the job or contract, then the employer or manager may be firm in taking the employee to task. But even here there is no excuse for *harassment*.

And no workplace conflict should be allowed to escalate or degenerate into a situation that facilitates bullying.

If you are a victim of bullying, please do not suffer in silence or let the bully off the hook. Apart from having the right not to be bullied at work, you have a moral obligation to expose the culprit SO THAT HE OR SHE WILL NOT GO ON TO BULLY OTHER INNOCENT WORKERS.

Make a plan of action. Get yourself a notebook and begin a diary. Carefully jot down everything that happens in relation to your experience…when and where the bullying occurs…the time…the words used…the actions undertaken by the bully.

When you feel you have sufficient evidence and a clear picture in your mind of what is happening, or has occurred, set about lodging a complaint with the appropriate authorities.

If you need help formulating the complaint, do seek and accept such help. There are people who specialise in that field who are there to advise. You can outline your situation to them in absolute confidentiality.

A tried and tested three-point plan of action for dealing with a bully in your workplace has brought relief and closure to many victims. Once you are sure you are being victimised or targeted by a bully you may pursue this course of action:

One. Accept that this **IS** bullying. Don't try to persuade yourself that you *deserve* what is happening or that the bully is somehow entitled to behave that way towards you. By recognising the problem for what it is, you will be less likely to suffer the sense of shame that some people feel if they become convinced that they have brought the bullying behaviour on themselves.

Two. Having identified the bullying as a wrongful act, you can proceed to the next stage…tackling the bully and looking after your mental and physical health that may be affected by the experience.

Privately see a doctor to establish if you are suffering from stress or anxiety brought on by the bullying. Consider also mental health counselling. Examine the code of ethics or behaviour that apply to your workplace and see if the bully is in breach of these rules or guidelines, or indeed of Labour law, or the civil or criminal laws of the land.

Three. Having noted the incidents of bullying in your diary, approach your employer and present the evidence to him, or, if your employer is the bully, go to the person who out-ranks him. If there is nobody higher up to approach, or if you feel you cannot trust anyone within the company or agency, see a solicitor and seek advice on how to proceed.

Whatever you do, don't just decide to suffer in silence. That is not an option…it is rather self-condemnation and the extension of a blank cheque to the bully to ill-treat, not only you, but others also.

Please…do not let your silence or lack of action become the springboard from which the bully can spread his evil behaviour to encompass other victims. Seek help. And record **<u>everything</u>** in that diary.

Remember what the Bible said: "Knock…and the door will be opened to you…seek and you will find…"

Pray to the Higher Spirit for courage and strength in your predicament.

And bear in mind…the bullies of this world will one day have to account for their actions when the Day of Reckoning arrives.

For your own part, wouldn't it be nice for you to be able, on Judgement Day, to recall that occasion back on earth when *you stood up to a bully*… thereby helping to make the workplace a less threatening environment for everybody?

Think about it!

☙

5

Angels and Spirit Guides

What is an angel?

Another frequently question. Angels are sometimes confused with spirit guides and ghosts, but are in fact different entities; though some of their tasks are similar.

You may remember at school learning a little prayer that went: "Oh Angel of God, My Guardian Dear". That referred to the Angel that looks out for you during your earth life.

Throughout history, reports of angels appear in literature, in the biographies of saints and mystics, in the Bible…and the sacred scripture of other religions.

Countless reports have been documented of people who claim to have seen angels or been helped in some way by them. Lives have been saved by angelic intervention.

Traditionally, artists have depicted them with wings, and against heavenly or celestial backdrops, singing the praise of God.

In modern times, newspapers and magazines worldwide carry "Angel Columns" devoted to aspects of Angelic life and what these wonderful beings can do to help us all in our earthly quest for meaning, fulfilment, and success.

Angel Cards are all the rage nowadays as a spiritual yearning for the true meaning of human existence draws many people, especially the young, towards the various methods of communicating with the Angelic realms.

But what are they, you may ask? Angels are beings that do not incarnate on the earth plane, but who can and do offer guidance and help to humanity, and have been doing this since time immemorial.

Interestingly the word *angel* derives from a Greek word Angelos, which translates as *Messenger*.

In occult and spiritualist literature, angels have been divided into nine categories: Seraphim, Cherubim, Thrones, Dominations, Virtues, Powers, Principalities, Archangels, and plain…*Angels*.

Another batch of angelic beings are the *elementals*…the nature spirits who guard the domain of the natural world.

They are better known as devas, sylphs, gnomes, salamanders, undines, and elves…the supposedly mythical but in fact very real "fairies".

So when you hear someone say of a man or woman: "Ah, he's away with the fairies", don't automatically dismiss the person being ridiculed, as he or she may indeed be attuning to higher levels of reality.

When you complete your earthly "endurance test", you will see angels of all kinds, including the much-maligned "fairies", and then you will know that nobody deserved to be frowned upon or gratuitously dismissed for being sensitive to the invisible world.

Angels move constantly among the inhabitants of the earthly realm, and although we may be unaware of their presence most of the time, they never cease giving us their loving and benevolent attention.

You may have seen an angel at some point in your life without realising it…bearing in mind that this resplendent being need not have wings or appear to be about to fly away, as angels can also assume human form, especially if and when they wish to come to the aid of a person in distress.

A Guardian Angel is one specifically assigned to each person throughout his or her lifetime. This angel watches over you, but will not undertake any undue intervention that would interfere with the accomplishment of your life-mission. You have to learn the lessons assigned to you in the School of Life.

The Guardian Angel will use all due discretion in determining if and when intervention in human affairs is justified or ultimately helpful to the person to whose care the angel has been entrusted.

So when you recall that childhood prayer, consider its true meaning: That prayer, or invocation, grew out of a well-founded belief in angels that has filtered through into many of the world's major and minor religious belief systems.

Whatever about its shortcomings, the priority accorded in the Christian faith to the role of angels on this earth and in the spirit realms is entirely appropriate…because angels are the eternal messengers of the Creator. They are there to comfort, and in the words of the prayer: "to watch and care, to rule and guide".

> Here is what Andrea Bonny has to say on this subject, in a poem honouring her sister Shelly:

Angels

Angels, are you playing?
Is my sister there?
Can you hear her laughing?
Flying through the air?

Can you tell my sister Shelly
That I miss her so...?
Tell her that I love her,
I know she had to go.

All you angels, playing,
Give comfort to us all...
Tell my sister Shelly
I love her most of all.

Andrea Bonny, Dublin.

Spirit Guides

Every one of you has a spirit guide. These are people on the Other Side who take on the task of helping and guiding us throughout our lives.

While many of them may never have incarnated on earth to experience the highs and lows of life down here, many others are people who once lived and loved and worked like ourselves on earth, and so have firsthand knowledge of the challenges and difficulties that we have to contend with.

These compassionate spirits receive the necessary training in the Spirit World to prepare them for working with us flesh and blood humans. They can then engage in the essential inter-dimensional assignments that characterise their life-enhancing, inspirational work with us.

A friend or relative of yours who has passed over may become a guide for you, and who better to give you a helping hand from the unseen world than someone who knew you in your earth life, who is aware of your strengths and weaknesses, your hopes and aspirations…your family circumstances?

In the same way that people here on earth specialise in one profession or line of activity, so also there are different kinds of spirit guides, each with a specific purpose or field of competence.

If, for example, you are a composer engaged in creating a musical composition, a guide with a background in music or who was a composer or musician in his or her earth incarnation might come to your assistance, to inspire you and give you that additional creative zest and energy to bring your work to completion.

Many writers have attested to sudden flashes of inspiration that made the difference between success and failure in their careers, or of receiving guidance in dreams that altered the course of their literary adventure for the better.

Here again, a spirit guide may be offering gentle and non-judgemental inspirational or motivating support.

Whatever your chosen path in life in terms of career or creative outlet, a guide with the relevant knowledge and understanding of your needs and abilities and potentialities will be there to lend a hidden hand to your efforts.

Another kind of guide will help with relationships, one of the most fraught and potentially painful and emotionally destructive areas of human existence. Very often, we ignore the promptings of our guide and enter a relationship that goes off the rails.

Better to meditate and reflect carefully on where we are going in a relationship than leap blindly into the unknown, taking risks with people we may know nothing about. We should not, however, think of even the most disastrous relationship as having been a complete waste of time. Nobody comes into your life by accident.

There is a definite purpose in all relationships and human inter-actions. Though we suffer the pain and heartache that go with the downside of relationships, we also learn from these. We grow, become wiser, and evolve spiritually as a result of all those knocks.

So don't blame your spirit guide if you end up in a relationship that turns sour. He may have seen further than you and realised the value of the "Lesson of Life" that you learn as a result.

Some spirit guides specialise in what we on earth think of as the medical field. Some of these may have been doctors themselves in their earth lives and now they work from the Spirit World, healing people with physical or mental ailments where possible by influencing via positive subtle intervention their auras and energy fields.

A Spirit Guide, when one can see him or her as a clairvoyant can, appears to us in any way that he or she prefers.

The clothing arrangement or hairstyle or other physical characteristics that you see are created out of spirit energy to correspond with how the guide *wishes to appear.*

Depending on which religion you adhere to, or were born into, a Guide may appear as a bishop, a Tibetan Monk, a nun, a wise man with a flowing beard, or indeed assume any appearance deemed appropriate in the circumstances.

One of my Guides is a Red Indian. Many spirit guides who have assisted mediums down the centuries were, in their earth lives, Native Americans. They were oppressed members of a deeply spiritual nation that succumbed to colonisation and all but disappeared as an ethnic group.

But in the world beyond they excel as highly evolved beings and are to the forefront in bridging the gulf that separates our two worlds.

A Guide will never interfere in your life in a judgemental manner, or suddenly appear in a flash of lightning to reprimand you for misbehaving, or anything like that. But he/she is aware of your circumstances and is always ready to help.

You need only ask for help in order to receive it. It may not manifest in exactly the way you envisage.

For example a Guide cannot do something you ask if it is unethical or would lead to harmful consequences for you or your fellow human beings.

A special type of Guide enters the equation when one happens to be a medium. This Guide is sometimes referred to in psychic literature as a "Gatekeeper", and for a very good reason.

When a medium goes into trance, this "Gatekeeper Guide" is there to protect him or her, to keep the medium safe from any negative spirit energies or entities that might attempt to invade the body of the medium while the "normal occupant" is facilitating communication between the Spirit World and clients waiting to hear from their loved ones.

6

What goes around comes around!

Though we must all face up to the consequences of our actions on the Other Side, there is no sadistic overlord waiting over there with a pitchfork and swishing tail to administer punishment.

The simplistic Heaven/Hell division of the afterlife as taught by conventional religions is far removed from the truth as perceived by those of us who can see into the Spirit World and communicate with its inhabitants.

Even the religions that once emphasised Hell so much have revised and amended that part of their teaching to some extent, realising perhaps that it could no longer be sustained and that it is not supported by the evidence that has come to light concerning the true nature of the spiritual dimensions that exist beyond the boundaries of our physical Universe.

For centuries this arbitrary black-and-white division held sway, with people who obeyed official religious teachings being signed up for the front seats in Heaven, while anyone who sinned or didn't go to mass supposedly got a one-way ticket to the Land of Fire and Brimstone.

What didn't make sense for many people who had to listen every Sunday and sometimes on weekdays to this terrifying oratory was the notion that a wise, compassionate, merciful God could be so cruel to humans when they died…sending them hurtling down into the flames of everlasting damnation.

Thankfully, we now have a more balanced, accurate, and enlightened understanding of the afterlife, due mainly to the work of psychic mediums and paranormal researchers.

As a medium, I know that the Spirit World is very different from that bleak place of extremes that the preachers of old dreamt about. It is a place of healing and joy, of continuous progress and limitless creativity.

Scientists will tell you that everything that exists is in motion…vibrating at a certain rate. The reason most people, apart from those with psychic perceptions, cannot see or hear the Spirit World is that it vibrates at a much higher rate than the physical world…and this applies also to those who have crossed over to that world or level of existence.

But when we die, and vacate our earthly bodies, we become part of that world, and quickly adjust to its living conditions. Temporary exceptions to this rule, as explained elsewhere in this book, are people who, of their own accord, refuse to "move on" and opt to remain on the earth plane…but these eventually see sense and cross to the Spirit World.

There to greet us on the Other Side will be our loved ones who went before us…family…friends…even pets we had back on earth. Among the people and entities to greet us will be specially assigned guides or helpers who enable us to settle into our new lives "over there".

These spirit beings offer us the necessary advice and guidance that we may need to adjust to life in the Spirit World. Our bodies in the Spirit World will be of a finer composition…no flesh or blood or bone…no risk of illness or disease…no need to eat or drink or sleep, unless you wish to engage in any of these human chores out of habit.

It doesn't matter what shape your earth body was at the time of physical death. In spirit you will have a healthy, pain-free body. Habitation won't cost you a cent, as money doesn't exist in the world beyond (there are no banks or stock exchanges or brown envelopes over there!) and the landscape is truly stunning, more beautiful than the most creatively ingenious depictions of Heaven and the Hereafter that our world's greatest painters have achieved.

Likewise the sounds: the music surpasses in serene melodious beauty any composition we have ever heard here on earth. Anything we have seen, heard, felt or otherwise experienced is but a pale reflection of what we can expect to perceive when we arrive in the Spirit World.

There are different levels or states of existence in the Spirit World. These are not separated by physical boundaries of the kind we see on earth. The level we occupy depends on our degree of progress on earth…the point of spiritual evolution to which we have attained throughout not just our most recent lifetime but over the course of all our earth lives.

So where's the catch, some of you will ask. There isn't any…but there is **accountability**. You do have to account for your life. Each of us has to undergo a cleansing process known as the "Life Review"…which in religion is referred to as the " Judgement Day".

We get to see and re-visit everything we have done in the earth life just ended…to consider our spiritual progress, or lack of it…***we see and feel the impact of our thoughts and actions on other people.***

This process brings home to us the message that **LOVE** is one of the greatest lessons of life on earth…that hurting other people, physically or mentally, is something we need to learn NOT TO DO.

Of course if you have devoted your earth life to committing horrendous crimes or making life miserable for other people you will have to pay the price…by not progressing to the higher levels of the Spirit World.

If you have led a truly evil existence, you will be effectively *holding yourself back*…because hatred and jealousy cannot exist in the higher states of being.

A speedy return to the earth plane to commence a new *more challenging* life could be on the cards for you if you are in that category…so that you may hopefully learn next time around NOT to behave that way towards your fellow human beings.

Affairs…

Something else I have found in my work as a medium is that, no matter how clever people think they are about concealing any form of wrongdoing or betrayal, it will always catch up with them at some point. If not here on earth, then certainly when they reach the Spirit World.

I don't mean that "Hell" in the old fashioned religious sense of the concept awaits them. But having to face up to the truth about ourselves, and ALL our actions, thoughts, and intentions, is a final reckoning that we should be aware of as we tread life's journey.

This principle applies across the whole spectrum of human behaviour. Take cheating in marriage or sexual partnerships for instance. This form of betrayal hurts deeply, and the person on the receiving end of it may go through life with a burden of bitterness and mistrust as a result.

Allow to me give a few examples that illustrate how futile it is to cheat on your wife, husband, or partner.

A woman who had cheated in her marriage on a regular basis came to me for a reading. As the channels of communication to the Spirit World opened, her husband made himself known and I had to tell the lady that he was present. To her shock and amazement, he grew emotional and accused her of cheating on him during his earthly existence.

She was aghast, because she had no idea that he knew, or could possibly have found out. What she failed to realise was that once he reached the Spirit World he had been informed of the infidelity and betrayal of trust. He was therefore fully aware of the secret affairs she had been conducting behind his back for many years of the marriage.

Startled by this revelation, and by the knowledge that her deceased husband had figured out the whole situation from the Other Side, she broke down crying and bawling. Tears flowed as she begged forgiveness of her husband.

This was difficult for him, but he forgave her, so both of them drew comfort and closure from this remarkable healing session. She had faced up to her shameful actions and accepted responsibility for these, and he had found peace and contentment due to her sincere apology.

I would stress here that such a forgiving attitude, whether you are here on earth or in the Spirit World, is essential if we are to move on and progress spiritually. Likewise accepting and facing up to our past wrongdoings is vital too if we are to evolve as beings healthy in mind and body.

The shoe, to quote the old adage, was on the other foot in another reading. Again, the client was a woman, but this time it was her deceased husband who was in for a jolly good and well-deserved reprimand. She knew he had cheated on her…by leaving money and property to his own family in his will and leaving her penniless.

When I announced his presence she asked me if he could actually hear her if she said something to him. When I confirmed that he could, she let fly…she released years of pent-up, suppressed anger and bitterness at how he had treated her. There was plenty of name-calling and recrimination.

He tried to apologise, saying he would act differently if given another chance. But of course it was too late for that. He couldn't change her hard-pressed financial or social predicament from the Other Side. There was intense emotion on both sides, she in my consultation room and he in his new home in the Spirit World, and an obvious need for the two of them to find closure, however difficult or painful this might prove.

I advised her to seek professional counselling to help come to terms with her situation, and I must emphasise that I always advise clients to get such help if they manifest signs of traumatic or stressful conditions that require conventional medical or psychiatric treatment or care.

Please bear in mind that people very often bring unresolved grievances with them across the Great Divide and into the Spirit World. So it is better to be fair and honest in all one's dealings with people, especially in relationships. Absolute trust and loyalty have to be the cornerstones of these sensitive human interactions that are so central to all our lives.

༺༻

7

Some Thoughts, Reflections, and Advice on Domestic Abuse…

As a medium, I deal with far more than the psychic and spiritual forces and arranging for people in the Spirit World to communicate with incarnate humans. I have to contend with the whole gamut of human emotions and life situations.

A day doesn't go by without someone telling me about difficulties in relationships, family problems, betrayals in love, or expressing their hopes or fears about new or budding romances. Some of the concerns brought to my attention I find to be more appropriate to other disciplines.

Whilst a medium can indeed offer a unique perspective on life's manifold challenges, there are occasion when I, and most genuine mediums, will make a judgement that the person involved needs other forms of professional help, such as psychiatric treatment, therapy, or counselling.

Such are the obvious potential dangers facing the person that one has to recommend professional help, while also of course availing of one's mediumistic ability to assist him or her along the road to healing and release from whatever physical, social, health-related, or psychological ailment is presenting itself.

However, some of the issues that arise are so important that I have decided to devote a chapter of this book to addressing these.

I do so in the knowledge and certainty that properly tackling these challenges to wholesome living and a true spiritual existence is an essential key to achieving one's purpose in life…and to protecting vulnerable people from the man-made evil that seeks to make life miserable for so many human beings.

One of the most common problems I hear about in my work is spousal abuse. This continues to afflict homes across the country, with lives being wrecked because of it.

Victims who fail to break free from the cycle of emotional or physical abuse at an early stage may suffer for decades from its effects.

Many a decent, healthy, and wholesome human being has been brought low by this scourge. And again, one must allude to the subject that just doesn't go away no matter what sphere of human interaction or behaviour we are discussing: *Suicide.*

Because some victims of persistent domestic abuse opt to quit the earth plane; seeing no other way out of the dark chamber of horrors into which their lives have been plunged.

We tend to think of abuse as something obvious and physical; but emotional abuse can be equally devastating in its immediate and long-term impact. It can leave scars that prove difficult to heal.

Abuse takes many forms, all of them odious and indefensible. You don't have to tolerate *any* of these threats to your mental and physical wellbeing.

Though many couples find true happiness and fulfilment, there is always the potential for spousal abuse in a marriage or relationship. Basically, this problem arises when either partner starts trying to control the other person or dominate his or her existence in an unhealthy, intimidating fashion.

The abuser can be devious, availing of multiple psychological weapons to break down your defences as part of the drive to achieve power over you. Any trick or threat or stratagem that serves this purpose will be employed: Your own fear, for example, if he senses that you are afraid.

Once he picks up your fear, he will build on it and feed it, hoping to force you to retreat deeper and deeper into yourself. Guilt is another emotion that plays into his hands.

Though *you* are not the one who has anything to feel guilty about, he will seek to make you feel small and ashamed of yourself. Any weakness or perceived weakness he will exploit in the insidious effort to dominate and own you body and soul.

He may threaten to inflict physical injury on you, or to hurt somebody close to you, or he may drop subtle hints as to what can happen to you if you don't "play his game" and allow his sick form of control to succeed.

The abuser's obsession to control his partner stems from a need to be in complete charge of every aspect of the relationship. They want to be in the driving seat at all times, the ones who make all the important decisions affecting you and your family.

They are not happy unless they have a master-slave arrangement in the home. The victim must obey them as a solider obeys his superior officer. They want to treat you like a child, or a lowly servant who has no power and no right of appeal whatsoever.

If you a victim of such a partner, he will regard you as his possession… as much his property as his car or his wristwatch.

Mindful of the possibility that you might be tempted to leave to escape his freakish attempt at dominating you, the abuser will try even harder to make you feel small and weak and worthless.

He reckons…if she feels that bad about herself, she won't be inclined to leave as she'll get an even worse deal elsewhere, that her only hope lies with accepting her fate as his possession and plaything.

This process of weakening a spousal abuse victim's resolve to leave can take many cruel and malicious forms…To humiliate her, he will do anything that helps to break her down…He will insult her at every opportunity, but in ways that justify himself and cause her to feel ashamed or somehow at fault…he may call her hurtful names…or in public or at social functions he may subtly offend her in front of others without appearing to have meant it.

All of this eats away at a victim's dignity and self-esteem. It is a corrosive process that can only damage her mental or physical health, or both, if allowed to continue.

Or the abuser may take steps to isolate his victim, to strengthen her sense of dependence on him. Some abusers prevent their partners from calling on friends or relatives…and force them to request permission from them before they undertake any contact with the outside world.

If the abuser suspects that you are planning to go to the guards, or elsewhere, for help, they may resort to more aggressive behaviour, like threatening to kill or harm you, or your children…or to make some outrageous false allegation about you in public that would utterly destroy your good name.

They may become very violent, smashing glass objects around the house, or grabbing you while looking ferocious to frighten you into not exposing them. However an abuser handles the situation, his aim is to ensure that the victim is left in no doubt that she will suffer if she defies him or tries to escape the toxic relationship.

Abusers can be quite complex characters. Some days they can be as sweet as apple pie…on others like demons on the loose.

And they may even apologise for time to time if they fear they have gone too far, or blame their behaviour on a bad day at the office. If they feel guilt after an abusive session, it is more likely to be rooted in *fear of being caught* and exposed for what they are than any real remorse about their actions or words.

An abuser may also swear that they will never do anything like that again, giving false hope to the victim that maybe he has changed and that the abuse won't be repeated. This is just a cynical tactic to buy time.

But invariably, they sink into deep denial… strive to somehow shift the blame back unto the victim…make her feel that it was really all her fault.

Actual physical violence in a relationship lends a greater urgency to the victim's need to escape the situation.

The physical abuser is extremely dangerous. If you are in a relationship with this person then have no doubt…your life is at constant risk.

This person is also devious, like his counterpart the abuser who confines himself to hurtful words and mind-games. He may of course combine the two…verbal attacks and physical assault, to show you who is boss in the home and assert his control.

Physical abuse involves a variety of brutal methods of assault including hitting with fists, half-choking, tossing household items at you, pointing a gun or knife or other potential weapon and threatening to use it.

Such behaviour is a crime under the law of the land no matter what excuse might be made concerning it being a "domestic row" gone wrong.

The violence may begin with a bit of pushing or shoving, or light slaps to "put you in your place", but then gradually escalate and worsen over time. The slaps turn to fully-fledged punches. The beatings can affect any and every part of the body, inflicting external or internal injuries.

The more devious abusers will try to avoid leaving marks on your face, knowing that these will become difficult to keep explaining away as bruises you have sustained from bumping into doors around the house.

The physical abuser is someone you need to escape from as soon as you possibly can, because tomorrow may be too late.

Research has shown that he tends to fantasise a lot about how he is going to keep you down. He devotes time to convincing himself that you deserve punishment and chastisement.

When he has worked himself into a frenzy with his fantasies and false images of you "failing to measure up" or "letting him down", he lashes out at you, feeling completely justified

Therapists and psychologists who have studied this dreadful problem have identified a pattern in the abuser's behaviour that seems to emerge repeatedly whenever a domestic violence case is brought to light: The abuser strikes his wife or partner. Shortly after, he may say "sorry" and express grudging regret for having struck her in what *seems like* remorse.

Therapists caution any person on the receiving end of this kind of scenario not to be taken in by this seeming apology. What the abuser is really saying, inwardly, is "I'd better say sorry in case she reports me".

He progresses from this point to fooling himself into believing that you are maybe cheating on him, having a secret affair, though he has no real evidence of any kind to support this notion.

But it reinforces his determination to excuse his actions to himself and justify his violence towards the victim. He starts scolding her with reprimands like: "you make me hit you with that attitude of yours" or "if you didn't carry on that way, I'd never hit you".

The false apologies continue, mingled with continuous violence. To feed his prejudice against the victim and his need to justify himself, he may deliberately set her up...like for example send her on a shopping errand and then, if she is later than expected, accuse her of having a secret lover.

Those never caught up in a domestic violence situation may find it difficult to understand…or even believe this…but the apologies that follow each abusive incident actually *succeed* in persuading many victims to remain in the relationship, hoping against hope that the suffering and the fear and the cruelty will cease.

So the cycle of violence goes on. The cuts and bruises heal, to be replaced later by more of the same, or maybe something worse. Victims have ended up in intensive care wards in hospitals, or on life support systems after bad beatings.

And some have been murdered, intentionally or otherwise, in cases where the abusers went "too far", even by their own twisted standards of what level of abuse is acceptable.

An abusive partner may also attempt to bully and control you by sexual abuse within the relationship. Surveys conducted in Ireland and the rest of Europe show that around a third of men who batter their wives also rape them at some point, often very violently.

Therapists warn that any situation involving unwanted, forced, or deliberately degrading sexual activity, within or outside marriage, constitutes sexual abuse and is a crime. They warn too that people that misuse sex in this way as part of their obsessive controlling behaviour are liable to kill or seriously injure their partners.

Warning Signs

If you feel you are in an abusive domestic situation but have doubts on that score, here are some questions you need to ask yourself:

Are you increasingly AFRAID of your husband or partner? Are you reluctant to raise particular subjects or concerns with him for fear that you will anger him?

Do you feel he is belittling or attempting to "dominate" you, as mentioned earlier?

Is he driving you into feelings of self-hatred and a growing sense of desperation or feelings of being trapped in a threatening situation?

Has your partner got you into a state of fearing that no matter what you do he won't be satisfied?

Has he managed to manoeuvre you into a state of mind where you accept that you *deserve* to be beaten, yelled at, verbally abused, or isolated from your friends and family?

Are you feeling emotionally helpless as a result of the kind of relationship you are in?

Does he constantly put down your every opinion or remark?

Does he treat you more as an object than a human being?

Is your partner's temper nasty and unpredictable?

Has he threatened you with violence at ANY time, or struck you physically even once?

Has he compelled you to engage in any sexual practises *against your will?*

Has he ever deliberately damaged or destroyed any of your personal possessions or any items in the home that mean a lot to you?

Does he manifest extreme jealousy or paranoia in relation to where you have been or whom you have been visiting?

Does he attempt to exert inordinate control over your finances, forcing you to account to him for every cent?

Does he seek to hurt you financially by withholding money you are entitled to?

Does he withhold any food, clothing, or medical necessities from you?

Does he try, by overt or devious means, to disrupt or sabotage your own career?

How to End the Suffering and the Nightmare?

WALK AWAY FROM IT…AND SEEK URGENT HELP!

You don't have to live with this nightmare. No matter how much you think you love him or how much you believe he loves you…you are entitled to a life. He has absolutely no right whatsoever to use you or your mind for emotional target practise.

Every couple has rows or arguments, and there are differences of opinion from time to time that need to be ironed out. But these issues can be dealt with on equal terms, and in a civilised way.

There is NO situation in which bullying or emotional abuse in a relationship is justified. It is always, without exception, a morally repugnant, cowardly, sinister, and mentally corrosive tactic. And whatever the domestic circumstances, or the background to the problem, you should never, if you are a victim of this abuse, blame yourself.

You are not to blame, regardless of what he has managed to imply via his clever mind games and unjust innuendos. If you ARE a victim of this sick behaviour, my advice to you is: Seek help immediately. Don't wait around in the hope that somehow he will change, or that deep down the guy is someone who really loves and cares for you.

If he *really* cared about you, he would not be wearing you down and putting you at risk of developing any one of a number of physical or mental illnesses that can result from prolonged exposure to this kind of harassment in the home.

If he is feeding on your fear, reach within yourself to find the *courage* that is the perfect antidote to fear. Make a clean break. Leave him. You don't have to tell him to his face that you are leaving if he is the type of person who might react violently and harm you

Remember: If physical violence is used, you may end up with cuts and bruises, or internal injuries. Such domestic assaults, affecting both men and women but mostly women, are all too common and both police and medical services believe they are under-reported.

Domestic violence can occur at any stage of a relationship…half way through…or at the point where the couple is close to splitting up.

A common misconception about spousal abusers is the belief that they have lost control of themselves or cannot curb their tempers.

In fact it is more likely to be the exact opposite scenario: The abuser is quite *consciously* using violence and intimidatary tactics to exercise control and break his partner.

Far from being the result of momentary impulses or a so-called "short fuse", domestic abuse is notoriously calculated and deliberate, a strategy designed to "put the victim in his or her place"…a choice freely taken to achieve the abuser's twisted ambition to turn his partner into a mere shell of a human being to be manipulated and managed and misused as he sees fit.

If you are a victim and doubt this, ask yourself…does he bully his workmates or anyone apart from you? Does he beat them up?

In nine cases out of ten the answer will be no. The spousal abuser isn't that kind of bully.

He doesn't target his victim when there are witnesses around. That's not his style. He does it in secret…with no one to see and hear the cries of his victim, or see her frightened expression.

He doesn't fight fair…he only abuses the one person in the world who really loves him…loves him so much that she can't accept the horrifying truth about the bully that lives in her house.

Abusers evolve shrewd ways of evading responsibility for their actions. They learn to appear convincing when they deny any allegation, and to appear angelic as if butter wouldn't melt in their mouths at the mere hint of wrongdoing.

For example, if the abuser is in full flight, in the process of giving his partner her daily or nightly dose of undeserved grief…and the phone suddenly rings…he can calmly pick it up and have a friendly normal conversation, as cool as a breeze, halting to laugh or chuckle or sigh gracefully at the right moments, and maybe even dropping casual references to his wonderful marriage or relationship.

Then, when he replaces the receiver, he is capable of resuming his cowardly attack on the person he feels he has a right to control and manipulate.

So please, don't give an abuser the benefit of the doubt. If you do, you are gambling on your own safety, possibly your life. Pick up the phone today if you are affected by domestic violence or bullying.

Waiting around for your partner to change is not just a waste of time. It's dangerous. Just be sure when you make contact with the Gardai or other authorities that he is not listening, or likely to see or hear you.

It's your life to enjoy and fulfil, not anyone else's. Nobody has the right to bully, beat, enslave, isolate, or manipulate you in your own home under any circumstances. So get out…act decisively to put your life back on track.

What if it's somebody else? Intervene!

Also, if you suspect that someone you know is a victim of domestic abuse, don't hesitate to call in the authorities. There are signs to watch out for that indicate the problem exists: Ask yourself…has your friend or neighbour been complaining quite a lot about unexplained "accidents" that caused marks or bruises?

Has she been absenting herself frequently from work? Have you noticed her reacting with fear or unusual nervousness in the company of her partner, or referring to his horrible temper or irrational anger in conversations?

Has she become unusually withdrawn from her former social circles, or from society generally?

Any obvious personality changes…or bouts of depression that she doesn't want to talk about? A noticeable lack of financial resources…at a time when the couple appear to be doing well financially?

If you have cause to suspect spousal abuse is talking place, call one of the confidential help lines or the Gardai and report your suspicions.

If you happen to have got it wrong, the authorities will take no action. But allowing the abuse to continue when you know or strongly suspect it is happening is not an option.

Always remember that you are here on this earth for a purpose. Every cause has an effect…no matter how much time elapses between them. If you become aware of an instance of spousal abuse and do nothing, you are failing in your duty towards your fellow human beings.

As well as deliberate crimes and violations of the moral law of the universe, there are "sins of omission"…in other words failing to act righteously when the opportunity presents itself makes you *partly responsible* for the continuation of the nightmare situation in that other's person's home.

So don't be afraid to pick up the phone…and think of that nice old Hebrew proverb: *"Whoever saves but one life has saved the whole world".*

8

Yes…it's happened to me too!

You might be asking yourself, after reading all this…how come she knows so much about these social, personal, and domestic issues that are not strictly relevant to the spiritual themes you expected to dominate the pages of this book?

Well, this might come as news to some of you, but mediums are, first and foremost, **human beings**. We experience the slings and arrows of misfortune, and life's joys, as much as anyone else.

We too know how it feels to be on the receiving end of betrayal in love and friendship, even more so in the cases of some mediums because being attuned to the higher, subtle spiritual energies and receptive to the voices of those who have passed over, we are naturally very sensitive to **all the emotions that underlie and characterise the human condition.**

Speaking for myself, I want to assure you that I am very much an ordinary person, with normal feelings and interests. Yes, I do have this extraordinary gift…a rare enough privilege…that enables me to access your loved ones in the Spirit World and convey tidings from them to you.

But this life-enhancing ability does not make me any less human or normal than the average man or woman who has not developed his or her psychic potential…any more than a brilliant surgeon or accountant or mechanic should be considered strange or "on the fringe" due to his or her devotion to any of these or other callings.

When I speak to you from these pages about betrayal, I am not merely broaching the issue from an academic standpoint, or citing the latest research. I speak, and write, from *bitter firsthand experience.*

In love and in friendships, I have borne the full crushing impact of the cruelty and vindictiveness that some human beings are capable of inflicting on their nearest and dearest. I have learned to my cost that there are some people in this world that simply cannot be trusted.

Certain lady friends who came to my home, and whom I welcomed with a hearty *cead mile falte* into my house, were happy to listen to advice and receive counsel from me. They confided in me and I in them…as one does with friends.

But these "friends" betrayed my confidence and made a mockery of what I had hoped and trusted would prove to be real friendship.

I marvel at the cunning and conniving ways of betrayers…the ones who play deadly mind-games behind your back…plotting and scheming… and in certain situations using your children or close relatives in cynical fashion to provide them with further information and material from which to mould even sharper daggers to facilitate back-stabbing.

Yes, dear readers, I have known the pain…the deep overwhelming sense of disillusionment that tears at the heart-strings and weakens your faith in the goodness of humanity.

And I can assure you, in spite of all that is rightly said and written about male abusers (within the home and outside it), that *women* can be every bit as devious when it comes to breaking your heart, or engaging in twisted stratagems to turn one's life into a pit of misery…whether they do it for amusement, or revenge, or out of jealousy or hatred.

I know that sickening feeling that comes over you when you discover that you've been cheated in life, which is why I understand the anger and pain experienced by the countless callers to my home who recount, tearfully and with acidic bitterness, how people they *thought they knew* pulled the proverbial rug from under them…left them reeling from the shock and the anguish of betrayal.

I ask such people to come to terms with their betrayal by a friend or partner…and *move on*.

There is nothing to be gained by sinking into a perpetual mind-numbing pit of self-recrimination…lamenting *what might have been* and endlessly recycling thoughts of regret and anger…fondly clinging to notions of what they would like to do to that person if they could get their hands on him or her.

Trust me when I say this…you hurt *nobody but yourself* when you indulge in such pointless ruminations. Negative thinking makes you a negative person. You merely give yourself illness, weaken your immune system, and stray from your true path in life.

Apart from hurting yourself, you run the risk of drawing other people in your family and in the family and extended families of the other person into what started out as a personal issue, thus widening the circle of heartache and inflaming the situation.

Some people who couldn't "let go" of the cheater have committed suicide, which, as I have emphasised in all my interviews and consultations, is **NEVER** a solution.

As with betrayers, so also with partners who want to end their relationships with you. **Don't stand in their way**. Respect their wishes…however painful letting go may prove to be.

Make a clean break. Put yourself in his or her place. If YOU wished to break off a relationship, would you want the other person to go berserk, or take revenge against you? Of course not…so respect *their* decision equally.

Bear in mind that all of us has a unique purpose in life, an individual path to travel and lessons to learn. Being your partner may not be part of that other person's life mission or plan. The proposed "parting of the ways" may have to do with his or her spiritual destiny.

You don't know *what* is motivating your partner in his or her desire to quit the romance or relationship. It could be that the two of you just don't "click"…or that you are not in harmony.

Or it could be that your partner has spotted another man or woman that he/she prefers. No matter. You have *nothing* to gain but heartache and a bucketful of misery by chasing shadows… and striving to cling on to *what is no longer there*. **Let them go, wish them well, and move on!**

Be careful too about any desire to "get even". No matter how one is wronged, revenge is *never* justified as a means of addressing the grievance. Revenge is a negative reaction that wreaks havoc in society. It may also hold up your spiritual progress after death.

Lashing out with violence, or engaging in the self-same destructive mental or physical assaults on people as you have endured is not the answer. You always seek *professional help*.

Fighting fire with fire only fans the flames of hatred and violence…and everyone gets burned, metaphorically speaking.

Here also I speak from experience, because I too have suffered the horrors of emotional and physical abuse at the hands of others in my life, and witnessed at close quarters the corrosive and corrupting evil of alcoholism.

If any *good* has come out of that personal brush with the dark side of human nature it is that I acquired thereby a greater understanding of what so many other people go through…it offered me an insight into the grim and terrifying emotional cauldron in which countless innocent victims of this crime continue to suffer in silence.

It has enabled me to reach out to victims in a way that mightn't have been possible had I had not myself known the pain, sorrow, heartache, and deep psychological wounds that one human being can so cruelly inflict on another.

I can empathise too with the pain of bereavement…of losing a loved one to any one of what Shakespeare called "the thousand natural ills that flesh is heir to". Death has claimed most of my family, and I know exactly what people go through when someone close is snatched from their midst.

But, being a medium, that sense of loss is tempered and soothed by the certain knowledge that the apparent "loss" is deceptive.

For what appears to the five-sensory human perception as a devastating loss…the banishment of somebody you loved, or cared for, or whose friendship you valued, is but a temporary absence on the time-scale of eternal life.

My mother, father, sister, and two brothers are all in the Spirit World…all very much *alive* in another level of existence with which I communicate almost every day in my work…and that I have seen with my clairvoyant vision.

I am the last of the family, though of course I have my own children and grandchildren.

I nursed most of my family at one time or another, and I knew real sorrow when consoling them after one of my brothers was murdered in England. I shared their pain, though thankfully I was privileged to know that he himself was at peace in the Spirit World.

And speaking of *being human*, I would remind people in the media that we psychics are as entitled to fair journalistic treatment as any other section of society.

This is an issue I must address because there are certain radio stations that have not, shall we say, lived up to the highest ethical standards of journalism in their approach to the work I do.

Elsewhere in this book I have written about bullying in its various nasty and debilitating forms. I regret to have to say that I have been subjected to bullying behaviour by a number of misguided radio interviewers. These were people who invited me on to speak about my work, invitations I gratefully accepted.

But once the interviews got underway it became evident that the person at the other end of the phone had no intention of "playing fair".

Instead of taking the subject seriously, these interviewers resorted to sarcasm and ridicule, making derisive remarks about an issue that is very serious indeed…the question of what happens to the human entity after death.

These so-called interviews turned into *interrogations*, with the people involved displaying their own prejudice and ignorance as they tied to discredit my work as a psychic.

This attitude, and this treatment of a guest, is totally unacceptable. It is character assassination, pure and simple.

They wouldn't get away with such lowbrow bullying tactics when interviewing accountants, doctors, politicians, or indeed people asked on to give their views on aspects of organised religion.

Believers in various forms of religion have been interviewed by those same broadcasters and never been subjected to the kind of gruelling that I have received. They were allowed to express themselves freely and without interruption and, in most cases, not asked any difficult or probing questions whatsoever.

There is, unfortunately, a hard core of deeply prejudiced individuals within the media who are clearly biased against psychics, who allow their own stresses, worries and personal problems to influence and contaminate their supposedly objective handling of radio interviews.

Interviewers have made unhelpful and inaccurate comments regarding how I deal with clients…suggesting that psychics generally take advantage of vulnerable people.

I can certainly clarify that in my own case I take no person who calls to me for granted. **Respect** is the keyword in all my work. If and when I consider that the person sitting in my consultation room has problems of a medical or psychiatric nature, I make a point of advising them to seek professional help.

I deal with the spiritual aspect, and while I do my best to facilitate the healing process, I always recommend that people see the relevant medical authorities or counselling services.

Apart from being unfair to me personally, such misrepresentation upsets many people who have put their trust in me. They hear the radio interviewer slagging off psychics, ridiculing what we do, laughing at the idea that there is an afterlife, and this undermines the healing process for them, especially if they are coping with bereavement.

The interviewers concerned have no idea of the harm they are causing and the hurt their gratuitously insulting attitude is having when they misrepresent some of the most vital issues facing humanity…the true purpose of life on earth and the reality of a world beyond this one.

One has to bear in mind that these are sensitive matters, literally of life and death. Consider the effect for example on a person contemplating suicide of hearing a radio interviewer snidely implying that nothing happens after death and that mediums are just performing a kind of circus act.

It is irresponsible in the extreme to turn a life and death issue into a subject for ridicule and mockery.

I would hasten to add that that these bullying broadcasters are in a minority. Many radio stations have interviewed me, both here in Ireland and in other countries, and I have also appeared on TV shows, and the overwhelming majority of the interviews were professionally handled.

I have the greatest respect for the people concerned. As an internationally known and accredited psychic medium I have a right to expect fair treatment in these situations.

In the past, people with psychic abilities were persecuted and, at the height of the religious extremism in Europe, tortured on the rack or burned at the stake.

We may have moved on since those dark days of ignorance and intolerance, but it does seem that certain groups and individuals with their own narrow agendas are determined to *continue* the persecution of anyone endowed with the rare gift to see or hear or otherwise perceive the spiritual realms.

Because they cannot themselves grasp the true significance of what lies beyond the range of ordinary human vision or hearing or perception, they lash out at those of us who can.

I urge these misguided people to re-think their attitude of hostility towards psychics and adopt an open-minded approach.

All I have asked for is a *fair hearing*, an opportunity to explain the work I do for the benefit of listeners to radio, viewers of TV, or readers of the print media.

I am not forcing my views on anyone, just speaking and writing *the truth* about my purpose in life, *which is to help others through my psychic readings and the healing power of mediumship.*

☙❧

A little poem composed by my mother Katie Geoghegan thirty-eight years ago for her grandson, Michael-John, after we returned to our home in England following a holiday with his Nan.

A Grandmother's Love

The day you went
I tried to be calm
But all I could see
Was your empty pram.

Your clothes were here
Your toys were there,
It made it very hard for me to bear.

I tried to keep them out sight
Before the long and lonely nights.
It would have been easier to bear
If your mammy hadn't left them there.

Katie

9

To Believe or not to Believe…

One of the oldest and most outworn clichés one hears from a sceptic when you broach the subject of life after death is: "Isn't it a wonder that no one ever came back to tell us what it's like over there?"

This throwaway remark is usually accompanied by a cynical smirk of derision or a knowing wink. The sceptic is so confident that he or she has closed the debate down before another word is spoken.

Death, the sceptic will tell you, is the end. Full stop. When you draw your last breath, you cease to exist. You're history.

Well, as a medium I am in a position to know just how false is that assertion of death equalling extinction. As for nobody having come back to tell us…I can personally vouch for the fact that they most certainly have come back…and continue to do so.

Not a day passes without the spirit of a "dead" person communicating with me or through me to attest to the reality of a "world elsewhere", a life beyond the grave that is every bit as real and solid as the one we currently inhabit. Apart from myself, mediums worldwide likewise are in regular contact with the world of spirit. They too are witnesses to the reality of dimensions beyond the earth plane.

Everyone is entitled to believe or disbelieve in an afterlife. That is their right, and I passionately believe in freedom of religious belief, and indeed in the right to disbelieve if that is one's choice. Free will is at the heart of our culture and democratic ethos in the Western World.

But for me, as a medium, scepticism is not a personal option when it to comes to a discussion on whether we survive death or not…because I know we do live on after the physical body expires. I know from literally seeing and hearing this great truth, of which I have been aware from an early age. And I earnestly wish to share that truth with the rest of humanity.

In my previous book, *Loved Ones, You're only a Whisper Away*, I recounted the story of my childhood psychic awakening, how as a very young girl I could see people in the family home and elsewhere that others could not see…of how at funerals I saw, in addition to the mourners and the priest in the graveyard…the liberated spirit of the body in the coffin about to be committed to the earth.

Many people have phoned, or called to my home, to tell me how comforting it was to read that. For me, it was simply an honest recollection of how I discovered my psychic abilities. I am glad that the book eased the pain of bereavement for readers.

I hope they are now coping better with their grief, knowing that the separation from their loved ones is only a temporary loss, that they will be re-united again at some point in the future.

The implications of accepting the reality of life after death are enormous for people who have sought to deny this fact. It means having to re-adjust their thinking and personal perspectives, re-ordering their concepts of living and dying to embrace the exciting evidence that mediumship provides of life everlasting.

And what a relief to know that yes, your loved ones really are alive… elsewhere…waiting for the moment that we too pass from this earthly existence to join them. I state this as a fact… not merely as an article of faith or an opinion I have arrived at by a process of conjecture or informed speculation.

When I say that we survive death, and that your dear friends and family members who have passed over are safe and content in the Spirit World, it is not just a platitude to console or make you feel better. It is an affirmation of absolute truth.

Scepticism is fine, and I respect it, but when you listen to the voices of real people who once walked this earth like you and me, and now inhabit another level of existence, then all doubts vanish.

Scepticism takes a nosedive when confronted by the powerful and irrefutable evidence of life after death that I contend with in my work as a psychic medium.

Sceptics ask derisively: where's the evidence for life after death?

For those of us who know the truth, no proof is required. We have the evidence of what we see, hear, and perceive via clairvoyance, clairaudience, and other extra-sensory means…we live the truth of mediumship every day of our lives.

But for anyone seeking evidence to support what we mediums already know and understand, there is a vast wealth of information and research findings out there that even the most hardened sceptic or atheist would find it difficult to ignore or brush aside.

There are many strands of evidence, any one of which on its own would be impressive and convincing enough…but that, when woven together into a complete presentation of the "case for survival", would convert any logical thinking person to a belief in what we mediums have always known to be true.

There is the evidence provided by mediums worldwide…information from a loved one in the Spirit World furnished by them that in many cases could not have been obtained by any other means…not even by telepathy or "mind-reading".

Such information, when given to a client who is unknown to the medium, is evidence of another state of existence wherein our dear friends and family members continue to reside.

The numerous sightings of ghostly entities by people from all walks of life also have to be considered.

The sightings of apparitions of the recently dead by friends or relatives.

Manifestations such as the stopping of clocks or pictures falling from walls when somebody dies…

Graphic descriptions of deathbed visions by dying people…when they clearly see loved ones encircle them…

Spirit photography, examples of which are included in this book, provide another of those strands of evidence.

Controlled, impeccably supervised experiments in which participating mediums passed on messages from the Spirit World containing information that could not possibly have been known to them.

Direct voice mediumship in which the actual voices of the spirit people are heard to speak during a séance and clearly identified by one or more of the people present as being the voices of deceased individuals known to them.

Many such séances were conducted under strictly supervised conditions to eliminate any possibility of trickery or fraud…and still the voices were heard.

Automatic writing, in which the hand of the psychic transcribes messages that are then analysed for their informational value. Such messages have also offered data that could not have been obtained by conventional means.

Reincarnation…if hypnotic regression shows that we lived before, there is no reason to doubt that we will live again…as the other strands of evidence already strongly indicate.

A form of evidence that has convinced former sceptics has been the so-called "cross-correspondence" messages from somebody in the Spirit World who, in his earth life, had devoted himself assiduously to psychic research and to proving that the human entity survived death.

Not surprisingly, he saw fit to continue with this important research… from the Other Side!

The fascinating story unfolded in the early twentieth century when a number of distinguished mediums in different parts of the world began to receive messages that appeared difficult to understand and somewhat cryptic.

Some were parts of sentences or fragments of lengthy quotations from literature. But a pattern emerged…a connecting factor in most of the messages was that they purported to emanate from Frederick Myers, the famous psychic researcher who had died a few years previously.

The various mediums each submitted the various messages that this spirit had given them and it transpired that the fragments fitted together to form a coherent message from him.

He had devised his experiment to rule out fraud or trickery on the part of any of the individual mediums he contacted from the Spirit World.

Each medium involved had no idea of the contents of the messages the others had received. It was only when the pieces were put together that the complete message could be deciphered and read.

Among the aspects of this trans-dimensional experiment that impressed psychic researchers was the way the personality of the spirit, Mr. Myers, came through so clearly in the transcript of the complete message.

This drew remarks from old friends of his such as "that's Myers alright", and others who had known him during his earthly existence also vouched for the seeming authenticity of his communication.

You can read detailed accounts of the great "cross-correspondence" experiment *conducted from the Spirit World* in the literature of psychic research and there are numerous Internet websites devoted to it.

A fair, unprejudiced, open-minded study of the evidence supporting a well-founded universal belief in the afterlife would convince any reasonable person of this great truth.

In my first book I mentioned that I had attended the world-renowned Arthur Findlay College in Essex, England, in my younger days when I was developing my mediumship.

It may surprise you to know that Arthur Findlay, the man in whose honour the college is named, was once a hardened sceptic himself!

It was only after his firsthand experience of a great Scottish medium, John Campbell Sloan, that he became profoundly interested in psychic research.

Seeing Mr. Sloan facilitate spirit communication and provide first class evidence of survival convinced Arthur Findlay that belief in an afterlife was no mere superstition, but an obvious fact of life.

I draw attention to these evidential points (which you can explore further for yourself) to show that this is a subject worthy of serious attention and consideration… to demonstrate that we are dealing here with real issues and a world beyond our earth plane that is not some vague shadowy or dreamy place…but a state of existence as real as the pages of this book or the walls of your house.

☙❧

10

Suicide…

A Tragedy that benefits none…and diminishes all

In my previous book, I drew attention to what many health experts and media commentators have dubbed "the great epidemic of modern times": Suicide.

Since then, many more people, the majority of them teenagers, have opted to end their earth lives by self-inflicted killing.

The processions of hearses followed by grief-stricken broken human beings continue to wend their sad course through the towns, cities, villages, and rural districts of this land. And the same questions are asked:

Why did he leave us like that, when he had everything going for him? Why did she take her beautiful young life in its prime…a whole life of promise and career prospects and friendships and fulfilment ahead of her?

The same irrepressible guilt too. The self-tormenting that afflicts loved ones who blame themselves for somehow letting them down…the feeling that if only…*if only.*

Why didn't we notice anything? they plead.

Why didn't we catch the signs, and why didn't we show more understanding of this precious much loved person who has so abruptly, so suddenly, been snatched from us?

September 10th each year is designated Suicide Prevention Day in Ireland. This year, as before, the occasion brought forth a myriad of heartbreaking tales of families torn apart by this tragedy…from every corner of the land their voices were heard on radio and TV, recalling the terrible, never to be forgotten moment they heard that a son or daughter or parent or sister or brother had been found, and how they felt when they read, with trembling hands and disbelieving eyes, the brief note offering what the suicide victim thought of as an "explanation" or a "reason".

But no reasoning or explaining on anyone's part can suffice to take away the heartache or the overwhelming sense of loss.

The causes of suicide are manifold, but depression has to come at the top of the list, and also a sense of despair or hopelessness brought on by the loss of a balanced perspective on life and its set of ordained challenges.

What happens, according to health experts who have studied this most harrowing of human tragedies, is that a person who commits suicide is utterly convinced at the moment he or she performs the act that there is really no other way out of whatever situation has led to the fateful decision to "end it all".

At that precise moment it seems the only option. The person wants to escape a given set of circumstances by cancelling out life…quenching the candle of existence. Then, they believe, they will cease to exist. And the problem or dark cloud that overhung them will disappear and be no more. That's what they believe.

Suicide does indeed *appear* to a person beset by seemingly insoluble problems to be the ultimate solution. But as a medium I have an absolute obligation to inform you that suicide is **never** a viable "way out" of life's more difficult patches.

I know from my personal knowledge and perception of the Spirit Realms that the supposed "quick fix" of self-killing is no solution at all.

Apart altogether from the bottomless pit of grief that a suicide creates for loved ones left behind on earth, this act of self-destruction destroys only the mortal body, leaving the spirit, and therefore the REAL YOU, completely intact.

So your attempt to bring about your own "extinction" will have failed. You can only destroy the body. You *cannot* kill the soul…which is the real "you".

After the noose has done its deadly work, or the overdose of tablets, or the water, or the bullet…you will have cast off the overcoat that is your physical body.

But you remain **alive** outside that now deceased mortal frame…living and aware and maybe wondering what on earth you have just done.

A person who commits suicide deserves our compassion and understanding. We are not here on earth to judge others.

But we *must* be firm and honest in pointing out to anyone contemplating an untimely departure from his or her earth life that this is **NOT a way out of anything.**

Of course a mentally ill or unstable person who dies by suicide is in a different category from one who takes the decision in a calculating or rational frame of mind.

A disturbing trend in recent years among young people who end their earth lives is the copycat syndrome whereby a teenager who sees all the attention and praise and sympathy lavished on a deceased friend or school mate develops an unhealthy obsession with receiving the same attention for himself or herself.

The emotional scenes at the funeral mass, with the priest tactfully complimenting the dearly departed, highlighting all the victim's good points, stressing that he or she will be sadly missed, etc. has a hypnotic effect on some teenagers.

They begin to crave this kind of emotionally-charged ritualistic send-off, with the whole community focused on that one coffin and that one person being mourned. There are some young people who *envy* the victim and this public concentration of awareness and newfound interest.

Again, I would appeal to anyone swept along on a tide of negative hero-worship generated by rituals and solemn words or catchy oratorical phrases: Stop and think…the person being mourned, that you see as being the centre of attention, is now elsewhere, safe and at peace certainly…but regretting very much that irreversible decision to "end it all". For, to repeat, you can't "end it all" by killing yourself.

You merely transfer from one world to another BEFORE YOUR TIME. So please, no matter what hand of cards life may have dealt you, remember that you are here to meet and overcome challenges, not to shirk them and leave this School of Life prematurely.

Let me tell you. What I say to you about suicide and why it is never a good option, or a solution, is not just my opinion. *It is my absolute knowledge, shared, I would add, by psychic mediums the world over.*

People like myself who are in contact with the afterlife all agree on that point: Suicide is never an option. Far from solving a problem, any problem, it yields but a harvest of tragedies. If you are contemplating suicide, seek help immediately.

Stop and think. Do you really want your nearest and dearest to be struck down by this unbearable burden of sorrow and unquenchable grief? Take the advice of people who *did* commit suicide and entered the Spirit World.

They *plead* with you not to go down that road, for your own sake and for the sake of those you would leave behind to mourn your passing.

On tapes, their voices have imprinted, expressing regret at their action and wishing they could undo it. You can make the right choice.

Seek help, and I promise that no matter how awful the situation you face or what obstacle you have to overcome, you'll cope and deal with it once you accept a helping hand from people who understand what is tormenting you.

The darkest hour is before the dawn. You don't have to cope alone and suffer in abject stultifying silence. Remember the old religious proverb: "Knock and the door will be opened to you…seek and you will find."

Being aware of the consequences of suicide on the spiritual as well as the physical plane levels, I implore anyone reading this to please *help* the quest to prevent this tragedy in any way you can.

Be vigilant. If you have any cause to suspect that someone you know, whether a family member or just someone you happen to know about, is contemplating suicide or might be suicidal, approach somebody close to that person you feel you can trust and tactfully express your concern.

Very often, a suicide victim will have left a trail of clues, however vague or subtle, pointing to his/her intentions.

Don't be afraid to intervene if you believe that something is amiss that might point in that direction.

Death Pacts

Another kind of suicide merits a more critical approach and consideration. This is the type wherein an entire family dies in what the media or local gossip construes to have been a "pact" agreed on by all concerned.

I must emphasise that from a spiritual point of view, if a man who is feeling suicidal decides to kill his wife and children also…in the belief that he has the right to "take them with him"…this man is guilty of murder.

He has no right, either in human law or the spiritual laws of the universe, to take the lives of those innocent ones. This fact will be made clear to him when he enters the Spirit World and his actions have the effect of holding up his progress in the afterlife.

You don't have the right to take anyone's life, and no amount of self-delusion or rationalising will get you off the hook if you commit this crime against a fellow human being.

I know from my mediumship just how dreadful and far-reaching are the effects of inter-family murders. When a husband kills a wife, or the wife kills a husband, there is a lot of reconciling to be achieved, on earth and in the Spirit World.

The family left behind has to cope with not only the loss of a loved one, but also the awful stigma that all too often attaches to murders of this kind. The children are left without parents, whether the parent who killed has taken his own life, or is arrested and ends up in prison.

The rumour and gossip mills creak into motion almost from the moment news of the murder filters out into the community. The children may be taunted at school as being the offspring of dysfunctional parents, especially if it was a murder and suicide double tragedy that has stricken them.

They may, if not helped and counselled very carefully and professionally, turn to drugs, alcohol, or extreme anti-social behaviour as a means of venting their sense of frustration, anger, and helplessness at what has befallen them.

They may rage for the rest of their lives against the unfair stigma that society has heaped upon them, or that they believe attaches to them. Meanwhile, in the Spirit World, the parent who was murdered is being helped by loving guides and angels, helped through a heaven-sent healing process to recover from the great wrong that he or she has suffered.

I find that most spirit people in that situation are anxious to know that their families back on earth are okay, and are getting the assistance they require and so desperately need to overcome the traumatic life-shattering ordeal into which the murder of a parent has plunged them.

In cases where both parents go to the Spirit World, one from murder and the other from suicide (having committed the murder), the murdered parent will of course be able to progress more easily to the higher levels than the one who has so cruelly ended his or her earth life.

The murderer has a lot of issues that have to be addressed, and it is in the lower levels that he or she must undergo the cleansing process that awaits all human beings who wreck innocent lives in this world.

As stated elsewhere, this is not Hell in the traditional sense, but a place of purgation essential to the purification of an entity before he or she can move on.

Earthly Justice…and Eternal Justice

On the subject of murder, I would remind readers too that the verdicts of courts on this earth have no bearing whatsoever on the spiritual reality of right and wrong that will be the only yardstick by which we are judged in the afterlife.

If, for example, a person commits a murder and, by artifice and top-notch legal representation, manages to convince a jury that he didn't do it, he will walk free from the court. The newspapers and television will proclaim his innocence, reflecting the official outcome of the legal proceedings.

But the matter doesn't end there. The court system can sometimes turn justice on its head, whitewashing the guilty in one instance and in another wrongly accusing an innocent man or woman of a crime they didn't commit.

There are some deeds that are grossly hurtful to people and yet not considered a crime under man-made laws. Betrayal is not a crime. Yet it causes more grief and hardship than any act of vandalism or shoplifting ever could.

Cheating on your partner is not a crime in civil or criminal law. But look at the havoc it brings to innocent victims of this reckless and selfish and irresponsible act? You can go to jail for not paying a TV license on time…but you won't spend an hour in a prison cell for cutting a wife or husband of your will and leaving them bereft and emotionally devastated.

But earthly justice is illusory. The day will come for all of us when we have to account for our true actions in life…not what we wish others to think we've done or haven't done.

The standards that apply here on this level of existence were created and are implemented by mortal human beings, often motivated or influenced by factors unrelated to any concept of right or wrong.

Legal experts and civil servants, at the behest of politicians, draft earthly laws. Those laws will always be flawed and unsatisfactory… blunt instruments that seek to more or less maintain a semblance of law and order in an imperfect world

When we arrive in the Spirit World, however, different standards apply. We are shown all our deeds, good and bad, and how these have impacted on the lives of others, for good or ill. We won't have a smirking solicitor standing beside us to play with words and sway a frowning judge perched up on a bench.

We will be confronted by the unvarnished truth…the full catalogue of our achievements and actions from the day we first drew breath as gurgling babies up to the moment we took leave of our earthly bodies. Nothing we have ever done will be hidden. All will be revealed.

Those who have led reasonably decent lives will have no difficulty with this purgative healing process. But anyone who has led a life marred by crime, hatred, sexual or spousal abuse of others, or insatiable greed, will have to face up to that negative life-record and take full responsibility for it.

Seeing and feeling the hurt we have inflicted on others brings it home to us how thoughtless and cruel we were to behave like that. Grasping the true significance of our behaviour enables us to purge ourselves of the nastiness that made such cruel behaviour possible.

But why wait until after death to face up to any badness within us? Why not strive *right now*, while we are still here on earth, to be better people...to substitute love for hatred, compassion for cynical unconcern, a spirit of generosity for rampant selfishness.

We must learn to accept that all life is sacred and that none of us has the right to cut short another person's allotted life span.

☙

11

Psychic Healing

Psychic healers are unfortunately too often dismissed as quacks in medical circles today. Yet for centuries they have used a combination of mental and physical medicines and practises to cure their patients.

In more recent times, the non-physical aspects of healing and medicine have been lost to much of mankind, with tragic consequences to people who could have fared better in their treatments were these additional options available to them.

Medical and scientific advancement swept away great swathes of the ancient wisdom and medical practise…the natural and psychic-healing methods utilised by the Shamans of old.

Of course modern healing techniques and practises did bring many benefits, eradicating diseases like Leprosy, Scarlet Fever, Plague, among other lethal threats to the health and wellbeing of mankind.

But sadly these advances also ushered in a burning hostility to the age-old psychic healing traditions that had preceded the age of modern medical technology.

To be fair to them, quite a few doctors today are willing to concede and accept the potentially crucial part a patient's mind can play in the process of recovery…and in slowing down the progress of, or even completely eliminating, a disease ravaging the physical body.

Abundant evidence has come to light to show that cancer patients for example live longer if they believe in their own ability to combat the disease rather than meekly giving in to it. Psychic healers specialise in tackling this aspect of treating illness.

They endeavour to heal the patients… by helping and encouraging them *to heal themselves*. Where possible, and in cases where a healer is endowed with a special gift, he or she many provide the psychic energy to boost the healing process in the body of the patient.

Increasing numbers of people are turning once again to these allegedly "non-scientific" methods of healing, realising that conventional medicine doesn't have all the answers and that, when modern cures don't work, it makes a lot of sense to try alternative means of effecting a cure.

When you opt for psychic healing, you are availing of forces that have been harnessed by men and women on earth for more than 50,000 years.

The Shamans of old were happily curing a multitude of human ailments long before the white-coated doctors and surgeons were ever heard of, and at a time when hospitals were non-existent.

They understood at a very deep level that the physical world was only one part of the universal reality, the other being the Spirit World and the unseen energy fields that swirled around every human and indeed and every object in the physical world.

They had discovered aeons ago that in order to comprehensively treat any illness you needed to take into account both the flesh-and-blood physical reality you saw before you AND the psychic energies that to most people were invisible but were equally relevant and deserving of attention if a healer was to address the true causes of illness and have a reasonable chance of curing the patient.

The more gifted Shamans, like the best psychic healers of today could pass with ease between the two worlds. They entered a trance and vacated their bodies temporarily, either to acquire special information or advice concerning an aliment in the Astral or to allow a spirit with specialised knowledge of the relevant illness or complaint to take over their physical body for the duration of whatever operation or curative procedure was about to take place.

Over the millennia, these natural healers made use of anything that could assist the healing process…laying on of hands to facilitate readjustment of energies, channelling of spirits, and of course the herbs and plants that they had found, by trial and error and exhaustive testing, to have curative properties.

The Shamans also found some of these herbs and plants to be effective in inducing trance or what scientists today call an "altered state of consciousness", the intention here being to enhance the healer's psychic ability and healing prowess, and facilitate a smoother line of communication with the higher dimensions.

In visions and out of the body states, the Shamans could receive vital messages from the Spirit and Astral worlds, in particular advice on how to treat illness…of both the body and the mind.

Twenty-first century holistic medicine is based largely on aspects of the Shamanistic approach to healing, which recognised that mind and body are essentially one, directly affecting each other throughout life on earth.

Many people nowadays opt to combine the ancient or alternative forms of healing with modern practises, resulting in the excellent concept of complimentary medicine that envisages an open-minded attitude to the use of all healing techniques.

While recognising the importance of modern conventional medicine, they realise that there are many instances in which a cure cannot be achieved by recourse to pill-popping, a stint in hospital, or going "under the knife" or the scalpel.

Unfortunately, there are still a lot of doctors and medical people generally who frown upon some of the more spiritually orientated methods of healing. They might grudgingly give the nod to the use of herbs, bone setting, homeopathy, or chiropractors…but tend to draw the line at faith healing or any method that involves interaction with the unseen worlds.

These narrow-minded medics dismiss faith healers and psychic surgeons as "quacks" and "witchdoctors", among other hurtful epithets used, and this is a profoundly unjust misrepresentation of what these wonderful people do to ease human suffering.

It is a grave and terrible wrong…this tarnishing of reputations that have stood the test of time and performance. If they would take the trouble to study and analyse the work of faith healers and the actual benefits of their healing techniques these sceptics might have a different view and perception of their valuable life-saving work.

Arigo-The Psychic Surgeon who defied medical science and cured thousands…

Among the many gifted psychics who have specialised in healing the sick was the great Brazilian, Arigo. He proved to believers and sceptics alike that the power of the mind can equal and even surpass that of the scalpel in the operating room.

In one of his first "operations", he was called to attend to a woman who was dying of cancer. Her family had gathered about her and she was expected to die at any moment.

Suddenly, Arigo dashed from the room in a daze, seemingly oblivious of his surroundings. Seconds later he returned…wielding a common kitchen knife. Stand back! He urged, signalling all present to clear away from the woman's bedside.

He immediately plunged the knife into the woman's body…to the alarm and bewilderment of the witnesses gathered around. He then inserted his hands into the gaping wound and pulled out a bloody tumour the size of a grapefruit.

Falling into a nearby chair, Arigo began to weep. The grieving family and relatives of the woman stood in mute shock, rooted to the spot. A doctor was called into the room. To the doctor's amazement, the woman was alive and smiling.

She was not suffering any pain whatsoever. The tumour was gone and there wasn't even any bleeding!

She recovered completely. News of this miracle cure spread like wildfire and Arigo was soon in demand across the length and breadth of his native Brazil and beyond.

People inundated his hometown…sufferers from every conceivable ailment in search of a cure. His healing sessions became legendary, and callers who observed him at work soon noticed that he seemed to be conducting his psychic operations while in a trance state.

Patients heard him speak in a different language that was confirmed to be German when he attended to their conditions. It emerged that Arigo, according to psychic researchers, was under the control and guidance of a German doctor who had died in 1918.

Any day he showed up at his surgery he could expect upwards of two hundred people awaiting treatment.

His methods would appear crude and brutal to any casual or uninformed observer.

He would push a person casually and forcefully up against a wall in his operating room and get to work on the patient right away with an unsterilised blade that could be a penknife or kitchen knife, or whatever he had handy.

Having completed the healing session, he quickly wiped the knife on his shirt and called in the next patient. Despite the lack of sanitation or sterilisation, patients experienced neither fear nor pain. Little or no blood remained after the operation and the wound healed almost instantly.

Throughout the 1950s and 60s, Arigo became a national hero in Brazil, performing an estimated fifty thousand operations over a five year period without ever accepting a single payment from a patient for his life-saving services.

People queued up to be treated for all kinds of illnesses and diseases and with a masterly flick of the penknife he ripped away the cancerous tumours or sliced out whatever was causing the complaint…and never once was any allegation of fraud or malpractice upheld against him.

He did however attract the hostile attention of conventional medical folk who took a serious dislike to his ability to heal people without recourse to normal hospital procedures. He was twice imprisoned at the behest of these negative elements that felt threatened and undermined by his success as a psychic healer.

On the first occasion he faced jail for his good work, the President of Brazil intervened on his behalf and granted him a Pardon, securing his release.

But then, the second time charges were proffered; Arigo was sentenced to several months in prison because the President who understood and supported his work was out of power.

Though he had committed no crime Arigo accepted his unjust confinement and used the prison term to help his fellow inmates. Incredibly, though he had been jailed for his psychic healing, the prison warders allowed him to operate on other prisoners and he saved the lives of many inmates.

Eventually, the legal system opted to give him a chance to prove that he really could cure people with his simple though seemingly crude method of healing. A senior Judge asked to be present to witness Arigo perform one of his operations.

A woman who was almost blind from cataracts on both eyes had agreed to let him operate on her.

Arigo requested the Judge to hold the woman's head while he performed the operation. The astonished judge later recalled what transpired: "I saw him pick up a pair of nail scissors. He wiped these in his shirtsleeves and he had no disinfectant of any kind.

"Then I saw him cut into the cornea of the patient's eye. She did not flinch although she was fully conscious. The cataract was out in a matter of seconds".

The Judge, and the District Attorney who stood next to him, were speechless. They noted that Arigo said some kind of prayer as he held a piece of cotton in his hand. A few drops of something suddenly appeared on the cotton and he wiped the woman's eyes.

"We saw this at close range. She was cured" the Judge recalled.

The Judge was convinced that Arigo was genuine…that he really was using a rare psychic gift to heal people. He did what he could within the strictures of the law to have the healer's sentence reduced, and Arigo was released after two months.

During the court case conventional doctors and other high ranking members of Brazil's medical profession had expressed their concerns about Arigo's work and methods.

They questioned prescriptions he gave to his patients, denouncing many of these as unreliable or dangerous. Yet nobody suffered as a result of Arigo's psychic healing or surgery…his patients had nothing but praise for him.

Arigo died in 1971. Though controversy still rages in medical circles as to exactly how he achieved his cures and healing, there is no disputing the fact that whatever force was involved, he did heal a variety of human ailments and that he operated with a simple non-surgical knife.

Equally certain is that he was under some form of exterior influence when he carried out his surgical healing…Observers claimed he appeared to be in a kind of daze when working.

Mediums and psychics the world over subscribe to the view that Arigo was indeed acting under the control and influence of a doctor in the Spirit World when he performed his life-saving operations.

Though an outstanding example of a psychic surgeon/healer, Arigo wasn't the only such medical prodigy in recent times. Today, the remarkable *John of God* is famed worldwide as a psychic healer.

In common with Arigo, he is based in Brazil and like his heroic predecessor; he enters the trance state and allows the spiritual influence to work through him.

John of God can call on the knowledge and medical expertise of more than three-dozen doctors in the Sprit World in his healing sessions.

I have personally seen this healer at work and can attest to his unique psychic gift, which has brought hope and a new lease of life to thousands of people around the world.

Absent Healing

While recommending such gifted healers to everyone, I would also emphasise that you should not neglect to see your local doctor if you feel your ailment is one that he or she can deal with adequately.

I recommend an open-minded approach whereby we look at both options…the conventional and the alternative or psychic forms of treatment. If one does not work, we can opt for the other.

Common sense and good judgement should prevail when making a decision as to which option is best for you. Don't allow anyone to pressurise you into accepting one or other form of treatment or healing. *You decide*, after due consideration and weighing up all the "pros" and "cons".

Of course one does not need to possess the extraordinary powers of people like Arigo or *John of God* to accomplish psychic or alternative healing. Reiki is another natural method of easing life's burden of pain and illness. It derives from a Japanese word meaning *Universal*.

It involves the laying on of hands and various pre-determined movements by the healer to readjust the invisible energies of the body in such a way as to undo energy blockages and remove the causes of ill health.

Where it cannot affect an absolute cure, Reiki may at least bring much-needed relief to the sufferer.

Some Reiki practitioners perform what is known as **Absent Healing**. This means they can bring healing to people who may be miles away, even on another continent. It must be remembered that time and space impose no limitations on the psychic healing process or on the healing potential of the spiritually awakened human mind.

Often, a *photograph* of the person seeking a cure or relief from an illness can be a valuable aid to the Absent Healer. It enables him or her to "make a connection" across time and space with the intended beneficiary of the healing process.

I have had people phone to tell me that I have sent healing to them, and this greatly pleases me because I am motivated in all my work as a psychic medium by a desire to heal the wounds of life.

Absent Healing is another wholesome way of bringing comfort and relief…especially to people with heavy crosses to bear on life's journey.

Respect the skills and professionalism of your GP!

A parting word on the importance of not turning away from your GP and the vital service he or she can provide. The conventional and alternative can co-exist in harmony, to the benefit of all of us.

In my readings I detect illnesses and allergies in people and will advise them to see a doctor to have their ailments looked into. It never ceases to disappoint me that some people won't go within a hundred miles of their GP when in fact they should be dropping into him for regular check-ups.

Part of the problem is an old belief that bad news greeted you whenever you saw a doctor, that it somehow presaged your imminent or impending death. This is a psychological hang-up that you need to get out of your system.

Men in particular can, I find, be very stubborn about caring for their health. Unless they are almost literally dying on their feet, they can't be persuaded to make that trip to the man or woman who can either tell them everything is okay, or what treatment will be required to set them on the road to recovery.

So please…forget the doom and gloom image of visiting your doctor. Take your courage in your hands and make an appointment to see him.

After all, you wouldn't think twice about having your car serviced or checked out every now and then for faults or mechanical failures. Yet that is just a machine, a metallic structure that has no life of its own. Your body is surely more important than your car.

It is the temple of the spirit, the vehicle you occupy for the duration of your earth life and as such you ought to treat it with the respect it deserves. You need to keep it intact so that you may complete your allotted span on earth. Think of your body as being "on loan" from your Creator. You have a duty to look after it, and you'll feel better if you do!

12

The Psychic Significance of Dreams

People want to know about dreams too. It's a subject that endlessly fascinates, because all of us dream, whether we remember our dreams or not. And the majority of us have several dreams in a night of sleeping.

Scientist will confirm that dreaming is essential to the normal functioning of the brain and have monitored sleeping in thousands of carefully staged experiments.

They claim to know when an observed sleeper is dreaming by monitoring changes to the patterns of his or her brainwaves and pulses and what they term Rapid Eye Movements.

But conventional science has never come up with any convincing explanation of what dreaming is, or of what exactly is happening to the human entity during this mysterious process.

That is partly because the non-spiritual approach of science and its strictly materialistic attitude to everything in the universe has made it difficult to tackle aspects of the non-physical world.

So the only theory that scientists really consider in relation to dreaming is the notion that the whole experience more or less stems from the brain of the physical body replaying images from life during sleep and maybe sorting through its memories and experiences.

But this explanation, while perhaps nicely accounting for a certain type of dream, does not come close to explaining so many others, certainly including precognitive dreams in which we get a preview of future happenings.

Of course you also can dream when awake…if not exactly *wide-awake*. This might surprise you…but laboratory experiments have established that all of us daydream for up to 120 minutes per day. This is a state of awareness hovering somewhere between being asleep and awake.

At school it was a big offence in the classroom if you were caught staring out the window, or thinking wistfully about anything not relevant to your lessons. Yet daydreaming is just another essential "safety valve" that we humans need to get by and cope with the material world.

We need those few precious breaks during the day when our imaginations run free.

Those who are that little bit more psychically gifted than the average person derive much benefit from allowing their minds to wander in this way, allowing their spirit guides or guardian angels to pass them messages as their minds open to subtle influences or inspirations from the higher spheres.

So never castigate anyone for daydreaming, unless perhaps it happens to be a man standing on the top of a building or tiling a roof, or a driver who should be watching the road. There's a time and a place for everything!

What is often referred to as lucid dreaming is a state of consciousness closely related to that one attains when out of the body or astral travelling (see chapter 15). In some cases, it involves the same phenomenon.

You find yourself in the middle of what looks and feels like a dream… but you are conscious. From that moment onwards you find you can *control* the dream and act as you wish in "dream-land"…except that very often you are not dreaming in the sense of merely fantasising or mentally reviewing the day's events…*you may have left your physical body during sleep and travelled to one of the astral spheres.*

Savour this experience if it comes to you. Explore the landscape around you and converse with the inhabitants if you encounter any. And, of course, be ready when you awaken in your bed to immediately jot down your memories of the experience.

You need to do this quickly, because your recollection of a lucid dream or astral journey will fade within minutes of you getting back to your physical body if you allow it to…like smoke flying out of a bottle…to melt into thin air.

Everyone has nightmares, and nobody likes them. More often than not, you will wake up feeling upset or frightened, or "out of sorts" at some point in this disturbing experience.

A nightmare can be a sign of some unresolved issue in your life that is crying out for resolution, or it could be a manifestation of a trauma or past event in your life that has affected you deeply.

In other chapters I have dealt with spousal abuse and bullying. These problems have spawned many a nightmare, as has posttraumatic stress, which can result from any traumatic event or distressful experience in your life.

If you have nightmares of a particularly disturbing nature most nights you might consider seeing a doctor or therapist, as these nocturnal ordeals have the potential to impair your mental or physical health over time, apart from the possibility that they are indications of other problems of which you may be unaware.

If you are struggling through a difficult relationship, or are dabbling in drugs or excessive drinking of alcohol, you can expect your fair share of nightmares.

Guilt is another cause…if you are hiding some dark secret from your past, or your conscience is bothering you because of some bad or evil act, again this guilt will visit you in nightmares.

If this is the case, you would be better off handing yourself in at your nearest Garda Station and owning up to whatever crime you are guilty of.

Though you may have to pay a price in civil or legal terms, you will at least have got it "off your chest" and should then enjoy a sound night's sleep…free from those nagging thoughts of guilt that either keep you awake at night or give you those nasty dreams.

Many criminals whose conscience forced them to surrender to the police admit the best night's sleep they had for years was after they were caught.

This is partly due to the balancing out of Karma…they are inwardly relieved that at least they are re-paying their debt to society, though they may not consciously feel that way or openly admit to the relief… and freedom from nightmares…that closure can bring to a man or woman with a newly cleansed conscience.

Another type of nightmare may feature malevolent or mischievous creatures of the lower astral realm. Many of these are not entities at all but merely powerful thought-forms that have been created by the hateful or ugly thoughts generated by humans over aeons of earth time.

The thought forms take on a half-life of their own and are attracted to people who debase their minds and bodies.

Again, abuse of drink or drugs can be the culprit here, sending your astral body hurtling on a downward spiral into the most debased and murkiest of the levels beyond the physical world. The famed "Pink Elephants" seen by drunkards are examples of such thought-forms.

While the best way to avoid such unpleasantness is to avoid narcotics and excessive drinking, if you do encounter intimidating astral figures while out of your body during sleep or drunkenness *do not show fear to these entities.*

They cannot harm you, but they can frighten you if you let them as they *thrive on fear*. Psychics advise you to face them squarely...don't run or try to walk away... and demand firmly that they depart.

If you are psychic, you may experience premonition in dreams. This means that you will glimpse futures events...before they happen. Non-psychic people can also receive previews of the future in this way.

Many people in the United States and other parts of the world had dream premonitions of the assassination of President Kennedy, which occurred in 1963. Dreams of disasters such as air crashes or the collapse of stock exchanges are quite common.

A number of people who had planned to travel aboard the Titanic on its maiden voyage from Belfast to New York had dreams in which they foresaw the ship sinking, so they cancelled their bookings.

From ancient times, people have dreamt of the future and indeed several famous men and women have been profoundly influenced by their dreams, some of them regarding these as warnings from the Spirit World or God. Dream messages have altered the course of history for both good and ill.

The Prophet Mohammed is said to have received a major portion of what came to be known as the Koran in dreams and he also interpreted the dreams of his followers, advising them of the significance of various symbols and portents.

Alexander the Great launched a big military venture; an attack on the city of Tyros, after interpreting a dream to mean such an attack was necessary and justified.

The great French martyr and heroine, Joan of Arc, who was burned at the stake after being wrongly accused of witchcraft, also received much of her inspiration in dreams. She believed God communicated his will to her in that way. In her dreams she saw herself liberating France from its enemies.

Napoleon Bonaparte, renowned for his military expertise, enacted all kinds of battlefield tactics and strategies in his dreams and, upon awakening, replicated what he had done while asleep on a model battlefield...and in some cases used the dream tactics to great effect in real life as Emperor of France.

During the Second World War, Hitler had a dream in which he felt himself suffocating amid collapsing masonry and stone. Upon awaking, he left the bunker he was in and minutes later it was blown to pieces by an exploding shell. The dream had saved his life.

Going back further in time, the Bible records many episodes of dream prophesy and interpretation. One of the best known is that of the Pharaoh's dream of the seven fat and thin cattle, and the seven fat and thin ears of corn.

He called upon Joseph to interpret the meaning of this dream. Joseph told the ruler that it meant there would be seven years of abundance in the land, followed by the same number of years of terrible famine.

And of course there is the episode, popular at Christmas time, concerning the dream in which Joseph and Mary are warned to flee danger. An angel appeared to Joseph in a dream to caution that they must escape King Herod or the infant would be murdered. Saint Peter had numerous dreams heralding future events.

Premonitions may occur at any stage within a dream, but some psychic researchers believe they are most likely during the "twilight" period... when you are still asleep and dreaming but just about to wake up.

They can also come during meditation or casual day dreaming...when the mind is receptive to spiritual influences and not too burdened by the chores and hassles of the earth plane.

If the same premonition comes to you in several dreams, this should be given special attention and noted carefully as it increases the likelihood of the prediction proving accurate.

For example, a psychic called John Williams dreamt in 1812 that the

Prime Minister of England would be shot...and that the shooting would occur in the lobby of the House of Commons in London.

He had this same dream several times and, true enough, the PM was shot in the parliament building as foreseen...within days of the final "dream warning" of the incident

As with any dream, you should write down anything that looks like a prophetic sign or signal or vision that comes to you during sleep, and then check it against actual events reported in the news that correspond to the dream images or premonitions.

A renowned old saying is that is that if you are confronted by a baffling and seemingly unsolvable problem...sleep on it!

This is sound advice because when you sleep and dream, forces from other dimensions come into play, in addition to the power of your own mind that is unfettered by conscious inhibitions and doubts that dominate the waking state.

Mathematicians, who may have spent endless hours trying to unravel some obscure, incredibly complex formula or code, racking their brains for weeks on end with no apparent prospect of success, have often found the elusive and much-desire solution in a dream.

Upon awakening, they immediately scribble it down...and celebrate!

Near Death Experiences of the kind mentioned elsewhere in this book may also occur in dreams...the dreamer in these situations can recall perhaps arriving in a splendid, beautifully illuminated place...a vividly hued landscape or inside a light-saturated building...where loved ones who have passed over may be present to greet him or her.

Or maybe a highly advanced being who advises that the dreamer has a crucial decision to make...whether to remain in this other world...or return to the reclining, sleeping mortal body to resume earth life.

The temptation to let go of one's physical plane existence and bask in the peace and harmony of this other world is so great as to almost overwhelming.

But, invariably, the great being who stands before you will advise you to complete your earthly life span, just as in the near death experiences I deal with in chapter 17.

A type of dream that bears some similarity to this is the one wherein you have a tremendously enlightening experience...what mystics call Cosmic Consciousness.

You may see your whole life in a flash and instantly understand at the deepest level the meaning of life...the purpose of all human existence.

Anyone who has undergone this magnificent, transcendent raising of awareness has always found it almost impossible to describe. Understandably, because no words devised by the human mind can describe the true spiritual truth that underlies all of creation.

For many who experience this "awakening in the midst of a dream", it is a life-changing insight into the glory of the Divine Order that sets them on a new, more spiritually orientated course.

They tend to become less selfish, abandon all thoughts of hate, greed, and over-weaning ambition, replacing these negative, cloying, destructive emotions with compassion and unconditional love for all their fellow human beings.

Not to be confused with a Near Death dream...which occurs when one has a "brush" with death but resumes life on the earth plane...is the dream of *approaching death*.

This may portend death of the physical body, but equally it may be symbolic in nature, pointing perhaps to an important transition period, or significant change in your life or living circumstances.

In a straightforward forewarning of actual death, you may receive reassurance from loved ones in the Spirit World concerning the great adventure that lies ahead.

From their exalted and happy perspective, they are in a perfect position to calm any fears or reservations you might have about exiting the earth plane and ascending to the painless transcendent world wherein they now dwell.

In the dream, which in this case is an actual encounter with real spirit people on the astral level, those wonderful friends and relatives who have passed over before you may explain via thoughts, images, or actual spoken words, what awaits you in Paradise.

You may perhaps be granted a vision of the Spirit World…a glimpse of what, after all, is but our true home…the shimmering towers and halls of learning…the multitudes of souls freed from pain and suffering…from the bleak shadowy earth plane where cruelty reigns and bullies thrive…where values are distorted and we struggle each day and night of our lives against the dark powers.

A death dream may be rich in symbolism. You may find yourself standing on a bridge suspended over a gentle stream in a tranquil setting…a radiant being on the other side of the bridge beckoning you to cross.

You might think there is something morbid about a death dream. But it has enormously positive potential: It enables you to make preparations, put your legal affairs in order, and maybe resolve outstanding disputes or quarrels.

And not forgetting that incredibly important duty…because it is an absolute duty…**YOUR WILL!**

The main purpose of the death dream may be to remind you that *drafting your last will and testament* in a fair and reasonable fashion is one of the great priorities of human existence.

It is not merely a chore or unpleasant task to be got "out of the way". How you approach this sensitive and demanding responsibility will have huge implications for those left behind on the earth plane.

I have explained elsewhere how unfair or maliciously drafted wills have caused untold suffering and resentment and bitterness, and led to family quarrels that have persisted for generations.

So if you are gently reminded in a dream that death may be near, make sure your will encompasses all those *who deserve to benefit from it*. Do not neglect a family member out of spite, an old grudge, or irrational hatred.

Always remember: If you use-or misuse-your will to hurt or punish others, you will be holding up your own progress in the Spirit World.

Then again… a "death" dream may have a more mundane interpretation. It can indicate a transformation in some aspect of your life…perhaps the ending of a relationship, which, when you think of it, can be a source of grief and mourning for what is passing away.

Or the dream may reflect your subconscious worries about a new departure in your daily work routine…maybe you are thinking of leaving your present job and starting in a new one. That represents one of the many "little deaths" that we all experience before the Big D approaches.

Or you may be on the brink of getting married…that too represents the "death" of your old lifestyle…the cosy family setting you were reared in…that you have known and grown accustomed to…and the commencement of married life with all its joys, woes, and manifold hidden dangers.

As with the Tarot, the symbols of death have many meanings, connotations, and nuances. The key point to understand is that death *always* implies change…whether to a new life in the Spirit World or to the next phase of your earth life.

Yet another kind of dream is the one that heals. If you are ill, healing may come from the higher planes while you sleep and dream.

This may take place in the physical body…but equally the healing may be effected in the energy body, bearing in mind that many ailments that afflict your mortal frame have their origins in invisible energy imbalances that conventional doctors tend to overlook because they are not trained to cure the spirit…just the outer form.

A healing dream may also come in the guise of a warning or advice from a higher being to you that your health is at risk and that you therefore need to see a doctor.

Certainly, if you dream about a specific part of your body being unhealthy or threatened in any way, do mention this concern to your doctor and ask for a check-up, though you don't need to tell him you got this warning in a dream!

If you are creative, dreaming can be a great source of inspiration for you. Even more so if you consciously decide to exploit your dreams and put them to good use. Many poets, writers, painters, and composers have drawn advantage from their dreams.

The English poet Samuel Taylor Coleridge was sound asleep when the words of his famous and most –often quoted and studied poem *Kubla Khan* came to him.

The evocative and haunting lines took shape in his mind as his physical body slept. But his spirit was wide-awake. Jumping out of bed, he reached for a pen and began writing it down. Unfortunately, before he had finishing transcribing all of it, a visitor called to his house.

This distraction upset his concentration and caused the memory of his dream to vanish, so he never managed to complete the poem. Still, the verses that he did recall stand as powerful testimony to the value of dream inspiration.

The famous-or infamous- book *Frankenstein*, about a mad scientist who created a monster and then lost control of him, was also a product of slumber-land.

Its author, Mary Shelly, wrote this masterpiece after waking up from a dream that featured all the essential elements that became the story she composed.

Robert Louis Stevenson's successful and influential *Dr. Jekyll and Mr. Hyde*, a novel about the power of evil, was also based largely on a series of dream images and events.

Painters have been influenced too by their dreams. The great Salvador Dali's works resemble actual dreams brought to life on the canvass, with their insights into the wildest flights of human fantasy.

On another level they can be seen as representations of the higher spiritual levels.

The Romantic painters often gave a dream-like quality to their work… with their Gardens of Eden…stunning ethereal scenery…hosts of angels and other supernatural imagery.

In the present day, there are psychic artists who paint with the greatest of ease what people instantly recognise as the "stuff of dreams"…in fact they are painting realistic and truthful scenes, images, and events, because what the sceptic regards as fantasy or illusion we psychics know to be very real.

Likewise, composers down through the ages have "made friends" with dreaming, realising that it afforded them the best opportunity to attune themselves to the "music of the spheres"…the melodies of Heaven itself that resonate in glory across the length and breadth of the Universe.

Having enjoyed the nocturnal bliss of these otherworldly symphonies of light and harmony, the sleepy composer wipes his eyes, gets out of bed, and, if he is wise, he will reach for pen and paper and scribble down the notes and scripts that have entered his dreaming psyche.

Needless to say, some of the best musical works ever composed were born in the minds of sleeping geniuses.

So, if you have any creative disposition or inclination, be sure to keep a writing pad beside your bed. You never know when a nifty or even world-shattering idea or inspiration may visit your dreams!

Abraham Lincoln and his Dreams

A man famed for his belief in the prophetic and healing power of dreams was Abraham Lincoln, one of the best loved of American presidents. Throughout his life, Lincoln had a deep faith in the existence of the Spirit World, and he tried with varying degrees of success to contact the dead.

Lincoln is renowned for his role in ending slavery, though the bloody Civil War that preceded this great reform grieved him, as he was by nature a peaceful man. He worked long hours and slept little, giving him those facial lines of exhaustion that show up so clearly in all the paintings and sculptures of him.

One of his first psychic experiences occurred during the 1860 American Presidential election.

After a long day of waiting for the result of the vote counting to be announced, he learned at midnight that he had been elected President. He returned to his home and lay down on a couch intending to sleep. Near the coach was a large mirror and something prompted him to gaze into it at his reflection.

Though sleepy, he was still awake when he saw a strange distortion of his mirror image forming in the glass. He saw his face reflected twice… one face was his own familiar self, but the second was paler and had what he described as *the colour of death*.

In the months that followed, this vision came to him again on several occasions. In later years, he interpreted the vision to mean that the healthy face indicated he would serve his first term as president… but the pale deathly image of himself portended that he would never live to serve a second term in the White House.

An event that affected him profoundly was the death of his young son William in 1862.

He was so crushed by this tragedy that he contemplated suicide, but instead turned increasingly to spiritualism

His wife Mary was a strong believer in communication with the Spirit World and in the course of Lincoln's presidency; many of America's most renowned mediums were guests at the White House.

A few of these are supposed to have warned the President that they had premonitions about his possible violent death. Lincoln accepted that the predictions were probably true, so he resolved to re-double his efforts to complete his mission in life.

For the remainder of his days he was convinced that the spirit of William was present in his office and his home. Some mediums were of the opinion that his obsession with William may have held the boy's spirit back, detaining his passing to the Other Side.

His wife Mary ensured that a regular flow of visitors with psychic abilities continued to call at the White House. One of them, a woman called Nettie Colburn Maynard held a séance at the world famous residence in 1863 at which a dramatic display of levitation was witnessed.

As the medium began to play a grand piano, it started to rise into the air. Among the observers was the President himself and a high-ranking military officer.

The President and the officer both tried to restrain the piano, by mounting it. But they had to jump off when it continued ascending and also began to shake and rattle. This incident convinced Lincoln beyond any doubt that supernatural forces were quite real and that there was a Spirit World.

But it was Lincoln's dream of his approaching death by assassination that has interested psychic researchers most of all.

Here is his own account of the dream, as related to friends: "About ten days ago, I retired late. I soon began to dream. There seemed to be a death-like stillness about me. Then I heard subdued sobs, as if a number of people were weeping. I thought I left my bed and wandered downstairs.

"There the silence was broken by the same pitiful sobbing, but the mourners were invisible. I went from room to room; no living person was in sight, but the same mournful sounds of distress met me as I passed along.

"It was light in all the rooms; every object was familiar to me, but where were all the people who were grieving as if their hearts would break? I was puzzled and alarmed. What could be the meaning of all this?

"Determined to find the cause of a state of things so mysterious and so shocking, I kept on until I arrived at the East Room, which I entered. Before me was a catafalque, on which rested a corpse wrapped in funeral vestments. Around it were stationed soldiers who were acting as guards; and there was a throng of people, some gazing mournfully upon the corpse, whose face was covered, others weeping pitifully.

" 'Who is dead in the White House?', I demanded of one of the soldiers. 'The President', was his answer, 'He was killed by an assassin.'

"Then came a loud burst of grief from the crowd, which awoke me from my dream. I slept no more that night; and although it was only a dream, I have been strangely annoyed by it ever since."

Less than a fortnight after this dream, John Wilkes Booth murdered the president while he was attending a play.

His body lay in state in the East Room of the White House, which had featured so ominously in the dream. Many people close to the president vouched for the accuracy of his premonition.

13

Earthbound Spirits…Ouija Boards… House Cleansing

People ask me: What is an earthbound spirit and why do some of us become earthbound after passing over?

When you die to the earth plane, you are free to "go towards the light" and enter the Spirit World to be with your loved ones and experience the joy and peace of that indescribably beautiful level of existence.

Earthbound spirits are temporarily denying themselves that peace and joy, of their own accord, and delaying their ascent to their true home.

I say *temporarily* because, no matter how long they chose to remain in this condition, they can move on at any juncture once they realise this is possible.

Once they accept this, a spirit guide will be there to help and advise, and also possibly people on earth with psychic ability.

I and other mediums try to help such people, and I will shortly explain some of the ways in which we do this. But first, let's have a look at how and why spirits sometimes remain earthbound.

A spirit becomes earthbound for any one of a number of reasons. They may not be aware that they have died to the earth plane and therefore insist on hanging around, instead of moving on to the next level of existence.

Or it may be that they were so content and happy in their earthly home or locality that they refuse to "let go", which they must do in order to reach their true home in the Spirit World where they can re-unite with loved ones and find a bliss and contentment far superior to anything they have known on earth.

So they remain behind, disembodied but bound by attachment or ignorance to a level they must vacate as it is not their appropriate dimension.

Such earthbound spirits account for many so-called hauntings, spectres, and ghostly manifestations, for those eerie houses and castles beloved of scary late night storytellers.

Most of them who stay on earth beyond their earthly lifespan are harmless to humans in that they intend no hurt or hostility, though of course anyone with sharpened sensitivity who happens to catch a glimpse of a wandering earthbound spirit may be frightened out of his wits.

Sometimes, a person who dies suddenly, perhaps in a traffic accident or heart attack or by violence will be disorientated for a while, being not fully aware that they have passed over so abruptly.

Seconds before, they were living, breathing human beings...then the sudden, unexpected changeover from earthly existence happens so fast its actual significance doesn't register.

They don't feel "dead"...because in spirit they are still very much alive, though without the mortal frame that for so long has encased their spiritual identity.

Confusion besets them, and they may try to speak to passers-by, but of course these cannot see or hear them owing to their spiritual essence not being visible to humans apart from those who, like myself, are clairvoyant and/or clairaudient.

A psychic present at the location of almost any sudden or unexpected death can perceive such spirits. Psychics on this side of the Great Divide, and spirit guides on the Other Side, endeavour to help these spirits to make the transition.

But they are free to ignore such help and advice if they wish. This, they find eventually, only holds up their progress and prolongs their habitation of a world they must leave behind.

Even when a spirit understands and accepts that the physical body has really died, it may still refuse to move on due to a fear of the afterlife it picked up during its earthly existence.

The ferocious and often sadistic sermons delivered from church pulpits may have imbued it with a completely unfounded and erroneous concept of what awaits the human entity after death.

The guides try to show them that they have nothing to fear, that earthly notions of hellfire and eternal damnation are pure invention…that judgement of the kind promised by fulminating clerics and ancient scriptures is very different from the true healing and non-judgemental nature of the Spirit World, and that though we must all account for our actions in life, none of us is condemned to an eternity of darkness or torture or isolation in some medieval chamber of horrors.

So fear holds them back, until they realise such fear is groundless, that there is nothing to fear but fear itself.

Yet other spirits linger on the earth plane out of a sense of duty. If a vital task or undertaking remained unaccomplished at the moment of death, they may feel an irresistible urge to hang around to "finish the job" or somehow ensure that the loose ends are properly tied up.

The spirit whose family is left in a precarious financial position may feel compelled to stay close to them, and not leave them behind and vulnerable by vacating the earth plane.

Or the spirit may become earthbound owing to a deep feeling of guilt or remorse. They can't bring themselves to move on until they make an effort to "atone", as they see it, for not looking after their families adequately.

Speaking in trance, I channelled a spirit whose message gave much food for thought. This was partly recorded on tape: Here is an extract: *"I am caught trapped…unnoticed…unable to change because I am without recognition…I am unloved. I am unseen by humans…I am powerless to move on without your help. Bring me into the world of light…of attention. Guide me on my path…"*

Yet another cause of failing to move on is over-attachment or addiction to drugs or alcohol. Their craving for unhealthy doses of these earthly substances holds them back.

They literally haunt pubs or wherever they can imbibe the fumes of alcohol so that, however disconcerting this might be to drinkers, ghosts may be sitting or standing or hovering close by in the pub, even it appears to be almost empty. The seemingly vacant bar stool to either side of you may have a ghost sitting on it.

Heavy drinkers when they pass over may refuse to "go towards the light" and savour the true joys of the afterlife and instead they may opt to delay the transition due to this deep-seated need to get their customary "fix".

Suicide victims too may linger, the shock and full impact of what they have done not having registered immediately. And the sense of remorse they feel about having left loved ones behind, grief-stricken and devastated, may draw them back to be with them in a bid to somehow comfort the newly bereaved family members or friends.

We on this side of the divide can also occasionally slow the progress of a deceased fellow human being. We may refuse to let him or her progress further by clinging to them in a way that keeps them earthbound.

We can cause problems if we allow our sense of loss spiral out of control…if it goes beyond the normal grieving and develops into an obsession. This can exercise a "pulling back" of the spirit who, out of concern for our mental state, may stay on the earth plane longer than necessary to comfort and console us.

People often misunderstand the status of earthbound spirits. It is important to bear in mind that they differ from those who have entered the Spirit World in the way the majority of us do after physical death.

When we return to the Spirit World in the normal manner, we receive healing for all the "slings and arrows" of the life just lived, or for any of the traumas or other suffering we have experienced on earth.

We also undergo the life-review in which we are shown how all our earthly actions and thoughts affected the lives of those we interacted with, whether for good or ill. This is a cleansing process and we are given guidance on how to progress further, having regard to our performance on the earth plane.

An earthbound spirit, however, because he or she has not gone through the life-review or the healing or cleansing process that go with it, is unhealthily attached to his/her old ways and habits.

Some earthbound spirits may attempt to strengthen their attachment to the earth by possessing living humans. This leads to disturbing consequences for the person affected and anyone who believes himself to be the victim of possession should seek the help of a psychic or spiritual healer who specialises in spiritual exorcising or cleansing.

Please do not confuse this with the over-the-top fictional depictions of hauntings and ghostly possessions in Hollywood movies. Sensationalist scriptwriters and filmmakers who know nothing of the real spiritual realms or the true nature of the afterlife produce these.

Unfortunately, such films create a distorted concept of psychic phenomena and the very important work that mediums do to bridge the gulf between the earth and spiritual dimensions.

The purpose of spiritual cleansing is to help what in past centuries and various cultures were referred to as "unclean spirits". The term unclean was meant to denote that these earthbound entities have not yet "gone towards the light" and made the full transition from this earthly level to the next.

House Cleansing

The good news for earthbound spirits and indeed for those affected or disturbed by their continued presence on earth is that we can help them make that "crossing" to the next level, thus removing the cause of the house disturbance or haunting that people fear so much.

Now, of course it may well be that you are happy to have such spirits remain in your immediate environment. You may be willing to tolerate them, especially if it becomes obvious to you that they mean no harm or are what one might call "benevolent spirits".

We are concerned here with disturbances that *do* upset householders. I have what is known as a house cleanser, whose function is to visit any home where unwanted psychic activity is reported. Upon entering the house, he has to establish the nature of the disturbance.

Please bare in mind that earthbound spirits may not be the source of a haunting or unwanted psychic manifestation. There may be dark energies in the house owing to a violent or traumatic incident that occurred on the premises at some point in the past.

If someone was murdered on that precise location, for example, a negative atmosphere might have carried over from that event.

But an all-too frequent cause of disturbances is the ill-advised and potentially quite dangerous misuse of the so-called Ouija board. I have been inundated in recent years by complaints and reports relating to the adverse effects of this activity.

I have always advised strongly against mindless or unsupervised dabbling in any aspect of the occult and I have seen the truly awful consequences of such interference by people who obviously haven't a clue as to the nature of the forces they are conjuring up.

The Ouija Board is used to contact spirit entities by uninformed people who hope to gain special knowledge about anything ranging from relationships, careers, or future events, to information about loved ones who have passed over.

Other people use it merely for fun, thinking it might provide them with a few laughs or a "Scare at Bedtime". They fail to realise its hideous dangers and that they are playing with fire.

Ouija is a mixture of the French and the German words for "yes". The board has the letters of the alphabet etched or printed on it and the numbers one to nine. The words YES and NO and the word "goodbye" also appear on it.

The sitters try to receive messages from the spirits by holding tightly to a glass that spells out the replies. To anyone experimenting with the Ouija for the first time, it may seem like a parlour game, an amusing diversion that might prove even more entertaining with a few bottles of beer or the odd snort of cocaine to add to the fun.

In fact, it is a recipe for mental illness, nervous breakdowns, and psychopathic behaviour. Some users of the board have never recovered from the experience.

Because I treat all clients in the strictest confidence, I cannot of course mention names. But I will give this example of how destructive the Ouija can be.

A few years ago there was a case in England that grabbed the headlines. The headmaster of a school in Essex was startled when a dozen terrified pupils, none older than fifteen, came racing into his office, blurting out a litany of shocks they had experienced after playing with an Ouija board.

Among the horror stories that greeted the headmaster were: the story of how a boy kept jumping up in his desk, swiping at spiritual entities that he claimed were bothering him.

He ran out of his classroom, shouting about a spirit that refused to get off his shoulder; a girl's claim that she could see malevolent dark entities in her bedroom; a boy's recollection of how a spirit tried to block his access to part of the school.

I have had the parents of boys and girls who dabbled in this and other forms of black magic come to me with tales of woe. But adults, who ought to know better, also fool around with these devices. There seems to be no end to the number of people who are prepared to risk their sanity by turning to this iniquitous and self-defeating activity.

My clear advice to anyone thinking of using an Ouija board is simple: Don't do it. Not under any circumstances. Any spirits you contact by this method will be of the lowest and most mischievous kind, and any spiritual energies you summon will be of the dark and malevolent variety.

These entities and energies may attach themselves to you, causing all sorts of unpleasant feelings, possibly depression and suicidal thoughts. If you mix alcohol with the process you run an even great risk of becoming unhinged.

A device not too unlike the Ouija in terms of the risk factor is the Planchette. This generally consists of a twin heart-shaped three-legged timber stand. Two of the legs protruding from it are on wheels while the third is actually a pencil or other writing implement with its point facing down.

The person using the Planchette places his hands on the wooden surface and then asks a spirit to move the device accordingly in order to produce written messages.

Though skilled mediums have in the past enabled spirits to indeed reproduce messages in the handwriting that was theirs in earth life, thus providing further proof of an afterlife for the sceptics, the problem with this device as with the Ouija Board is that it is wide open to abuse.

When used by people who have little understanding of the occult, or who combine its use with drink or drugs, it can open up the user to dark forces, and then, of course, people like myself are left to undo the damage wrought by this reckless behaviour.

When a house cleanser is called to a home, he has no idea of what he is up against until he walks through the door. Depending upon the nature and intensity of the disturbance or presence, he may have a relatively easy task on his hands or an immensely challenging one.

Some disturbances, especially those occasioned by ignorant dabbling in the occult of the kind just described, could present him with a difficult assignment.

There are cases where the house cleanser finds himself battling dark and extremely nasty elements that have been created or unleashed by such meddling.

He may emerge from such a confrontation with these dark forces covered in scratches and bruises…a reminder that what is involved here is very real.

Helping earthbound spirits in their transition is different, and gentle persuasion may achieve the desired result as such spirits are held back more by ignorance and misunderstanding or attachment than by any desire to do harm.

The cleanser has to be well protected for his task. Spirit guides afford him a measure of protection, but still, the process of banishing the dark forces can leave him exhausted and depleted. It can be a most demanding and draining ordeal.

One visit to the house may be enough to complete the cleansing. Or he may have to return and perform further sessions before cleansing is complete.

While the house-cleansers and mediums like myself are willing to help anyone afflicted by dark forces, I would caution that we are only human and there are limits to our patience!

There are what I might term "repeat offenders" when it comes to dabbling in black magic. You do your best to cleanse their home and then, maybe a few weeks later, the same person returns with a similar complaint…they have repeated the very practise you have pleaded with them to cease and reject.

They complain once again of depression, illness either mental or physical, menacing apparitions, and the most distressful nightmares.

If people are going to persist in conjuring negative energies then we of the psychic and mediumistic professions reserve the right to decline any request to visit these homes.

These people have been duly warned of the dangers, and if they refuse to listen, they will have to live with the consequences.

Think of it this way: You wouldn't let someone with no medical expertise walk into the operating theatre of a hospital and commence brain surgery on a patient. Or allow a person with no knowledge of mechanics to take your car apart and put it back together again.

And yet, the dangers implicit in tampering unguided in the occult can be just as dangerous. You could lose your sanity.

What price a healthy mind? You decide!

14

Tolerance and Prejudice…the Challenge of "Otherness"

Among the people of all ages and ethnic groups that come to me for readings are members of the Gay and Lesbian communities. Naturally, since at any time a considerable percentage of the population of any country, including Ireland, is Gay or Lesbian.

Some readers, upon reading this may say: Oh dear, that crowd, why mention them? Couldn't you leave those people out? In fact, that would be a mild reaction compared to that of so many Irish citizens when confronted by a sexual orientation and lifestyle of which they disapprove.

Because make no mistake: despite all the progress we have made in this country in terms of equality legislation and recognising the rights of all our citizens, there remains a powerful attitude of hostility, suspicion, and even hatred towards Gays and Lesbians.

I feel compelled to speak out on this, having listened to countless decent, inoffensive human beings who have suffered terribly as a result of discrimination and ill-treatment.

They have been misunderstood, bullied, called vicious hurtful names, and subjected to public humiliation by people who ought to know better. Each day can be a crucifixion for them.

Their only crime is to have been born with an orientation that some narrow-minded individuals cannot accept, owing to their blindness and prejudice.

So let me make it clear to everyone reading this: There is nothing remotely wrong or unnatural or inappropriate or unchristian or inhuman about being Gay or Lesbian, anymore than there is anything amiss about being a Catholic, Moslem, Jew, Hindu, Baptist, or a member of any given political party or organisation.

As a medium, I am aware of the reasons behind certain apparent life choices and human orientations. I see these from an altogether different angle than would the average non-psychic person. I would like to share with you my knowledge of the spiritual forces at work relevant to the Gay and Lesbian way of life.

To many so-called "straight" people, the very idea of a man being attracted to another man, or of a woman having a female love partner, is anathema.

They cannot fathom it. It baffles them and fills them with fear. And what people fear they may seek to remove or destroy. Hence the aggression, intolerance, and violence displayed towards Gays and Lesbians throughout the ages.

So why or how it is then, some readers will ask, that a person can be attracted to one of his or her own gender? The answer, which I give from my knowledge of the Spirit World's interaction with the earth world, may come as a surprise to you: Gays and Lesbians are not attracted to members of *their own* sex at all!

Let me explain…we are born into this world of physical matter, as I've mentioned before, to learn certain lessons or to accomplish a specific task.

Thus, for example, my own essential life mission revolves around helping people via my psychic abilities, another person may have to acquire the experience of living in a police state, or a broken home, coping with addiction, or he or she may incarnate for the purpose of campaigning for social justice, running a large household, overcoming prejudice, comforting the elderly…the list of possible tasks or life-objectives is endless

We come to earth for all sorts of reasons and with many good intentions. But it does happen that a spirit who is male and seeks birth into this physical world may find himself occupying a female body.

His psyche is still male but his "outer form" throughout life will be that of a girl and later, a woman. So quite naturally, he will be attracted to women…despite the fact that he is temporarily trapped or confined in a woman's body.

Likewise with a female spirit incarnating through a male body. She will be attracted to men, despite herself having the physical appearance of a boy or a man.

What matters for any person who finds himself or herself in this life situation is not the "outer form" or appearance…but the inner identity; the real being that resides within the earthly form.

Yet other Gays and Lesbians may have *chosen* to be born in a body of the opposite gender in order to experience the ups and downs of that very lifestyle and orientation. It must be remembered that the principal reason we come to earth is to learn lessons *that cannot be learned in the Spirit World.*

Think of the earth world as a life-long "boot camp", wherein you learn a variety of lessons essential to spiritual evolution and growth by a combination of love, kindness, and bitter first hand experience.

Apart from natural Gayness there are of course situations that engender or inculcate a homosexual orientation in a man or woman against that person's will.

In prisons, notoriously, men deprived of female company may become so frustrated and unfulfilled sexually in a twenty-four hour per day enforced male environment that they will, in desperation, turn to settling for what they believe or hope will be a temporary non-heterosexual relationship with one or more men who share their predicament.

Where such interactions or relationships are consensual, one cannot condemn or judge the people concerned, but unfortunately there is a high incidence of abuse in prisons and this must never be confused with the issue of being gay or otherwise.

Rape or sexual abuse is never acceptable, regardless of the circumstances or of what excuse is tendered by the person guilty of this most awful crime. It can destroy a person for life, and the victim may need years of counselling to help him or her to cope with the resulting trauma.

The abuse of people in that situation has nothing to do with being Gay or Heterosexual. Abuse is always wrong because it is an attack on the other human being that leaves him or her shattered and distraught.

To anyone out there who holds a deep prejudice against Gays or Lesbians, I appeal to you. **Stop and think**. These are your fellow human beings. You could just as easily have been born in the body of the opposite sex, and indeed it may be your assigned life mission to undergo that very experience in your next earth incarnation!

Try to empathise, try to understand why your brothers and sisters in the Gay and Lesbian communities have a different perspective on life, love, and happiness.

Hatred, mistrust, and negative suspicion based on fear or ignorance will have no place in the Spirit World that awaits you after life's journey ends. Neither should it have any place in your heart as you walk this earth.

The recitation of suffering and pain endured by Gays and Lesbians I have listened to over the years has been heartbreaking. One hears of Gay men who, to please parents and keep up appearances, opt to marry a woman for whom they have no feelings of love or affection whatsoever.

They may even have children, and maintain all the outer façade of a conventional heterosexual relationship. They feel compelled to live a complete lie, to feign emotions that are alien and unknown to them, suffering in silence as they strive every day to preserve that false front they present to society.

Eventually, the Gay man in that situation will find that he just can't take the pretence and deception anymore and just has to end a relationship that he knows is undermining his existence and tearing his heart to shreds.

Likewise with a woman who marries a man despite being Lesbian. She has to reach a point where she accepts her true identity and then she can seek out the kind of relationship that will bring her real happiness and fulfilment.

I would appeal to parents who have cause to believe they have a Gay or Lesbian child…do not punish these children, do not try to enforce your own concept of the ideal boy or girl on the child.

Do not threaten, as many parents have done down through the centuries, to have the child ostracised or banished from the home unless they "straighten out". Instead, support them, and talk to them frankly about their situation.

If you become aware that they are being bullied, or discriminated against, in any way, at school or by their peers, intervene decisively to confront that bullying.

Schools should make an effort to educate all children about the dangers of prejudice and intolerance, and emphasise that all children are entitled to equal respect and fair treatment, both from adults and other children.

The need to respect differences should be stressed as an absolute priority at all levels of primary and secondary school.

A Lesson from History

To remind you of where prejudice, intolerance, and fear-based persecution can lead, I would remind you of how another generation of human beings behaved towards Gays and Lesbians when tolerance, justice, and mutual understanding were pushed aside…and the bigots let loose…

You have probably heard of the infamous attempt by the Nazis back in the 1930s and 1940s to eradicate all ethnic groups and individuals who didn't fit in with their ideal of a perfect society.

Their most heinous actions were directed against the Jews, million of whom were wrongfully imprisoned and murdered just for being Jewish.

Every year, in many countries around the world, people commemorate that terrible chapter in the history of the human race.

What you don't hear so much about however is that Gays and Lesbians were also victims of the Nazi horror. Upon taking office in Germany in 1933, Hitler banned every group dedicated to helping or offering moral support to these people.

In the months previous to this, the German Gay community was at least tolerated, and it thrived in some of the larger cities of Germany.

But then, the Nazis decided that Gays should be treated as second-class citizens, and ostracised from the rest of society. The police raided their homes, and many were rounded up and sent to concentration camps.

The blind, unreasoning hatred and prejudice of the authorities, coupled with the silent but equally deep-rooted prejudice of the common people, condemned the Gays and Lesbians of Germany and much of Europe to cruel imprisonment and death.

In the camps, they were forced to wear armbands with pink triangles to identify and stigmatise them as being Gay. Camp guards routinely abused them, both verbally with constant name-calling and physically by means of the numerous tortures devised to make their lives hell on earth.

More than a hundred thousand Gays and Lesbians were arrested, and an unknown percentage of these died in captivity, many by gassing… others by hunger, exhaustion, disease, or brutal beatings.

Doctors were permitted to enter the camps to perform medical experiments on them without anaesthetic. Some of the experiments were designed to transform them from being men into women or vice versa.

The fate of one Lesbian woman, Henny Schermann, will serve to illustrate the end result of the kind of prejudice born of ignorance that has afflicted such people for centuries and that continues to this day:

The German police in Frankfurt arrested Henny in 1940 on suspicion of being a Lesbian.

When she admitted under interrogation to being Gay she was verbally abused by her interrogators, treated as the worst brand of criminal, and sent to a concentration camp.

After a brief spell in the camp, she was taken to the psychiatric wing where she was gassed to death. Henny wondered what her crime was. She had done nothing wrong, just loved another woman.

Henny was of course innocent of any real crime, just as Gays and Lesbians today are equally blameless.

But the fear and ignorance and suspicion that led to Henny and thousands like her being martyred by the Nazis is no different from that which still militates against the Gay Community today.

So next time you hear someone speak of the Holocaust, and what the Nazis did to the Jews, remember that they had turned their murderous hatred towards the Gays and Lesbians in their midst *before* they got around to targeting other minority groupings.

There should be a special commemorative event held each year in Ireland and elsewhere to recall the struggle for recognition and equality of Gays and Lesbians. After all, we have functions to honour our "patriot dead", victims of famine, soldiers killed in foreign wars, and the achievements of artists, writers, and politicians.

A similar public event to pay tribute to the courage of people who fought against overwhelming odds for "Gay Rights" would be entirely fitting and is, I think, long overdue.

Nobody should ever suffer the fate of Henny Schermann. No human being should have to endure mental or physical torment just for being Gay. I would hope that anyone reading this who in the past has harboured feelings of contempt or hostility towards Gays or Lesbians will abandon such negative, destructive emotions and leanings.

The admonition *Live and Let Live* applies especially in this instance. These are our fellow travellers on life's journey. We should respect and uphold their basic human and civil rights and, if we become aware of discrimination or injustice directed at them, we have a moral obligation to expose this.

Sex changes…Transvestism.

Here again, I urge absolute tolerance and understanding, because many people affected by these issues are in situations similar to those that confront and challenge Gays and Lesbians.

People who have undergone, or are planning to undergo, sex changes, have come to me for spiritual advice and readings. They sit before me, perplexed, feeling unloved, misunderstood, isolated.

I see and sense the awful pain of rejection and intolerance they have endured, much of it driven and fuelled by the same ignorance that has fanned the flames of prejudice for centuries against minority groups and lifestyles.

Some of them, I discover, have been banished from their homes and told never to return. Others have suffered, from an early age, a relentless barrage of taunting and cruel persecution from their peers, who cannot fathom or comprehend the true nature of the complex life-situation they see before them.

And, as already mentioned, what human beings fear and mistrust, they are impelled to put down, persecute, or destroy, as with the Nazis and bullies of all kinds.

To families who have a child, male or female, who expresses a strong inclination to exhibit the characteristics of the opposite sex, I say, please try to appreciate what is happening…and consider for a moment that the burden that fellow human being is shouldering in his or her earth life could just as easily have been your burden or life challenge.

You might also have found yourself in the wrong body, and now be coping with the difficulties your son or daughter or brother or sister is grappling with. Indeed you may very well be assigned that Lesson of Life for one of your future incarnations on earth.

So it behoves all of us to show compassion and unconditional love to anyone out there, whether within our own families or in society generally, who has been accorded that most demanding earth assignment.

People who actively persecute Transvestites, Gays or Lesbians would be prime candidates for future assignments as one or other of these orientations, and quite appropriately, in order to experience the very lifestyle or orientation they have failed to understand or tolerate or respect this time around.

The Law of Karma that one hears about so much in psychic literature apples in all life situations and could be summed up neatly in the common axiom cited in the title of chapter six "What goes around comes around".

Today's persecutor runs the risk of becoming a future victim of that same persecution. Today's bully may himself feel the pain of humiliation and fear-generated distress at a future date.

Therefore, do not seek to hurt or injure or put down people whose lifestyles or sexual orientations are not to your liking. They are here on this earth to experience life from that particular angle or perspective, and what they learn about themselves and others through that sometimes painful but nonetheless fulfilling assignment facilitates their spiritual evolution and growth.

Just as surely, those of you who are not Lesbian or Gay or Transvestite have a special responsibility in life to accept these brothers and sisters. An essential part of your life assignment is to avoid judging these good people or making life miserable for them.

Yet another point that has to be made concerns the person himself or herself who feels the need for a sex change. Do not deny to yourselves your real identity. You have the right to be true to yourself and to be who and what you really are.

You don't have to live up to anyone else's expectations or to any conventional or socially acceptable concept of what is deemed normal.

There have been cases where people who knew they were transsexual or inclining strongly towards becoming a member of the opposite gender have tried to suppress that inner truth.

Instead of accepting their true orientation, they opted to cover it up and, in some unfortunate instances, to condemn or publicly attack other Transvestites or Gays or Lesbians in order to divert attention away from any realisation of their own sexual identity.

An extreme example of how this kind of denial can get dangerously out of hand was the case of J. Edgar Hoover, the head of the American FBI. Throughout his long career as a top-notch upholder of State Security and the Rule of Law, he never lost an opportunity to condemn and savagely criticise Gays and Lesbians.

Though not quite as ruthless in his pursuit of them as the Hitler regime in Germany, Mr. Hoover authorised his agents to be merciless in tracking down any suspected criminal who had Gay or Lesbian leanings.

At dinner parties, press conferences, police functions and other public events, he lashed out at homosexuality whenever he got the chance. People wondered why he hated them so much. What had they ever done to him to elicit such prejudice and outrage from him?

The truth about J Edgar Hoover's supposed prejudice against Gays and Lesbians only emerged after his death.

His wife revealed that she had caught him several times, when he wasn't aware of her presence, dressing up in frocks and ladies underwear in front of a mirror in their home, and at one point she found a large assortment of women's clothing that he had been secretly putting on throughout the years of their marriage.

In other words, this man who was so outspoken in his condemnation of homosexuality appears likely to have been either Gay or Transsexual himself.

It was his denial of his true identity and his terror of being discovered by a society that he feared wouldn't understand; that drove him to persecute people whose orientation was similar to his own.

In retrospect, J Edgar Hoover too deserves our compassion, because it was society's ignorance and prejudice that compelled this man to suppress his true calling in life and turn his fear of being misunderstood into a negative, hate-filled agenda that hurt a lot of Gays and Lesbians worldwide.

Remember, nobody is perfect, and that indeed perfection cannot exist on this earth except as an ideal or aspiration.

Only in the higher spheres of being in the Spirit World can we find perfection. Here on Earth, we have to live as best we can together.

My message to you from the Spirit World and from the depths of my own heart is: **CELEBRATE** difference it…**DON'T JUDGE IT.**

You don't have to quench someone else's light to let your own light shine.

15

Astral...or "Out of the Body" travelling.

You may have heard or read stories about the Astral Body, and out of body experiences...not just the ones that accompany Near Dear encounters, but separation of the physical and non-physical bodies *while a person is still fully conscious and in perfect health.*

To understand how and why this happens we must expand our awareness of the great spiritual realities that conventional science either overlooks or would prefer we didn't talk about.

We need to accept and understand that in addition to our normal visible flesh-and-blood body we have other bodies, each co-existing with the others throughout our lives on earth.

When we shed the physical body at death, our consciousness simply switches or transfers to these other bodies, and we continue to live as before but without the now defunct and unoccupied body that we have discarded.

The more subtle but nonetheless real counterparts to our physical "frame", according to the teachings and findings of psychics and mediums worldwide, are the Etheric, Astral, and Spiritual bodies.

The Etheric is basically a body of energy, which, like the physical, is dispensed with at death. The Spiritual body is essentially the one we "slip into" after death when we enter the Spirit World.

But throughout our life on earth, we can leave the physical body and travel far and wide in what spiritualists and psychics refer to as the Astral Body.

This is an exact replica of the physical body, and when seen "on its travels" by a clairvoyant is immediately recognisable if he or she happens to know the person.

When we sleep at night, our consciousness transfers to the Astral Body and we can roam the earth safely in that "double", or visit friends who may also be out of their physical bodies.

Indeed, Astral meetings of this kind are becoming increasingly popular in recent years, with people arranging to see trusted friends or relatives on the "neutral ground" of the Astral state.

The problem with Astral travelling *during sleep* is that, while everyone does it, few people can remember precisely who they have seen or spoken to, or exactly where they have been.

You can overcome this drawback by asserting to yourself at night before you drop off that you will recall upon awakening all that has transpired. Otherwise, your memories will be disjointed…or mixed up with dreams and other mental cogitations of the mind.

If you wish to get out of your body while fully conscious, as distinct from waiting for sleep to overtake you, you can accomplish this by following a very simple set of instructions.

Here is one method: As you lie in bed, visualise yourself rising out of your body. Will it to happen. Think of a form gradually taking shape over you.

Practise this routine a few times…eventually, it could be the second or third occasion or it may take a little longer…you will feel yourself rising above your physical body.

It is very crucial at this point NOT TO PANIC. If you do, you will be pulled immediately back into your physical body with a jolt, such as that you experience when your Astral returns abruptly sometimes when you are drifting off to sleep. So don't panic.

Remain calm and allow the process to continue. If you hold your nerve and stay relaxed, you will float above your body and then, gently, alight to stand there in the room beside your bed to see your physical form reclining safely…breathing and maybe shifting about in the usual way as in sleep.

Having achieved this result, you may decide to return to your body, that you've accomplished enough for that session. But next time you can explore further. You could, for example, explore your house while in your Astral body. See what other people are doing and then tell them afterwards!

You will find that walls and other apparent solid obstacles do not impede your progress…you can literally walk through walls…and rise through ceilings. How is this possible, you ask?

Bear in mind that everything is composed of atoms and molecules… The Astral body is composed of finer material than your physical one. In the same way that water can seep into a bowl of sugar or microwaves can pass through glass, so also can the Astral form, which is lighter than air, pass through what we think of as solid objects here on earth.

People ask too: If the astral body is real, why doesn't everyone see it, instead of just psychics? One could say the same about the air we breathe, which is also invisible but composed, like everything else, of atoms and molecules.

The Astral is equally real. A Clairvoyant sees it simply because he or she has *heightened perceptions* and perceives with spiritual rather than physical sight.

Though not being impeded by solid objects, you may experience a slight tingling sensation when passing through these.

One very necessary and vital precaution you must take if undertaking conscious Astral travel is to ensure that you will **_not be disturbed_** during the exercise.

As already mentioned, any overt distraction will pull you back abruptly to your mortal body, and this can be quite an unpleasant sensation. Some people have likened it to a mild electric shock.

To avoid any such unpleasantness, take care that nobody will disturb you, and that you won't be distracted either by phones or doorbells ringing or visitors calling.

Spiritualists and psychic researchers believe that the Astral body is itself discarded, like the physical body at death, once we progress unto higher levels in the afterlife and thus occupy a body of greater purity and spirituality.

But on earth, we can avail of the opportunity if we so desire to leave our physical bodies and visit any location we wish in our Astral bodies.

In addition to visiting people and places on the earth plane, we can rise higher and explore the other levels of existence beyond the physical. There are ascending levels of being or states of existence that all of us will become familiar with when we die to this world.

But we can make "courtesy calls" to these higher worlds while still "in the flesh". How far up the scale of these higher levels we can reach depends on our degree of spiritual evolution.

A low-minded fellow addicted to drugs or excessive drinking of alcohol would be unable to soar into the bliss of the exalted states of being.

Instead, he might find himself on the lower levels…where mischievous entities, negative energies, and the most debased thought projections of humanity hold sway.

You may have heard of men on the mythical "Skid Row" claiming to have seen Pink Elephants and other phantasmal forms after a hard night's drinking and carousing.

Such people are languishing in the lower depths of the Astral. They must kick the habit and reform their addictive ways before their "trips" out of the body become wholesome and enjoyable…rather than an ordeal to be feared and avoided.

If you *do* happen to see any grotesque forms or creatures when out of the body, remember that these thrive on fear. Many of them are just thought-forms made up of all the nasty and hateful thought-projections of humans over the centuries.

They have taken on a half-life of their own, but cannot harm you unless you give in to their intimidating antics. Because they occupy the lowest levels of the Astral, you may never encounter them at all, but if you do, you can banish them with pure thoughts or by asking the Higher Spirit for protection.

Spiritually minded people, or those who live decent, wholesome, unselfish lives can ascend to the more exalted levels. There is no grim guardian or authority figure preventing us from entering the higher levels.

Only our own mindsets and limitations hold us back, just as in life we often restrict our progress by our own behaviour and attitudes.

Making contact with the so-called dead is one of the greatest benefits of the Astral experience. Psychics regard the Astral Plane as "the meeting ground between matter and spirit".

If you awake from what has struck you as an especially vivid dream in which you speak to, or see, a deceased loved one, this could be a memory of a real encounter with that person on the Astral plane.

What happens is that you, in your out of the body state, are able to meet the other person in a place or state of being that is amenable to both spirits and incarnate humans.

Your loved one can descend from his or her world to the Astral Plane, and you, for your part, may take a metaphorical "step upwards" to that same level…and you can then meet on this suitable common ground.

Communication at this level between humans still alive on earth and those of us who have crossed to the Spirit World is very common, with not a night passing without those loved ones greeting their friends and relatives who "drop in" during sleep to the Astral plane.

Again, however, as with conscious Astral travel in the physical world, you can quite *consciously* enter the non-physical Astral plane to meet loved ones if you wish, though this necessitates much training and practise.

Meditation is a favoured method of achieving this conscious projection of the Astral body. In my own case, I have received valuable insights and indeed spiritual messages while meditating.

As an intriguing "aside" to this topic, I must tell you that people have phoned to say they have seen me in various places at times when I was at home, probably sleeping or in meditation. One person apparently saw me appear in her house all in white!

These good people may well have spotted me in my Astral body… travelling quietly through the land while my physical form was resting…maybe after another day's work as a medium in the Spirit Room at Bennettsbridge.

☙

16

Neglect and Abuse in the Twilight Years

Another grievance brought to my attention in the course of my work has been the dreadful abuse of people in their latter years.

Elderly people, many of whom have contributed significantly to the creation of the new prosperous nation that Ireland has become, are cruelly victimised, subjected to neglect, ill-treatment, verbal abuse and bullying.

This is a sad fact of modern life in Ireland. Despite all our progress and the improvements in health care we have witnessed in recent decades, this scandal continues to shame our country.

Over the years I have had elderly people call to me to tell of their plight. They recounted how they had been subjected to horrendous abuse in their homes by close relatives…sons…daughters…in-laws, people who ought to know better and in fact be looking out for their wellbeing.

Instead, these younger family members make the lives of their older folk so miserable and unbearable that many of the victims tell me they wish they could die.

I have seen, and heard, grown men and women who were in their twilight years break down and weep as they described how their offspring, to which they devoted so much love and care and affection in the past…turned against them.

A man could be sitting by the fireside, reading the newspaper...when another member of the household suddenly grabs it from him without permission, with utter contempt. Or he could be ordered to clear out of the room he is in because visitors are coming.

He...or she...might be called vicious names or made to feel small and insignificant by these house bullies who are their own flesh and blood. Senior citizens are conned out of money, given the cold shoulder, pushed aside like refuse, treated like outcasts.

It often happens that an elderly parent who is in the family home is deemed to be in "the way" when a son or daughter marries and a "new order" replaces the former family routine in the house.

If the "grandfather" or "grandmother" by the fireside cannot be persuaded to leave...or check into a nursing home...his offspring, aided perhaps by the in-laws, may embark upon a sustained and quite deliberate campaign of overt or subtle pressure tactics to intimidate the unwanted tenant to get out.

They will stop at nothing in their efforts to force the departure of that "obstacle" to their ideal of the perfect home. There was a time when the older members of a family remained in their homes for as long as they wished. Their wishes were respected.

After all, they had brought those young people into the world, reared them, fed them, paid for their education; watched over them throughout the difficult trials and tribulations of childhood and the teenage years.

In return, they have every right to expect at least to be treated as living, breathing human beings with certain rights...including the right to a home free of bullying and threats and violence.

But certain families appear oblivious to their needs and human rights. Far from "honouring their father and mother", as obligated by the Ten Commandments of God, they transform what should be their happy twilight years of reflection and rest...into an undeserved penance.

These victims of abuse in the home far too often suffer in silence. They don't complain or speak out…partly because they mightn't be believed but also out of a misguided if understandable fear of landing the culprits in trouble.

Alone at night, they cry into their pillows. They plead with God and the angels in Heaven to ease their plight. They ask for nothing more than to be relieved of this torment.

They have asked me if their loved ones in the Spirit World could somehow come and take them…rescue them from the hell that their earth lives have become thanks to those cynical, uncaring, selfish younger ones who cannot seem to grasp the evil, despicable nature of what they are doing.

Apart from members of one's own family, guardians brought in from outside the family circle may victimise the elderly or infirm in the home. Care has to be taken to ensure that the man or woman receiving care of this kind is in good hands.

Reasonable checks should be run on anyone employed or assigned to look after an elderly member of any family. Just as you wouldn't entrust your personal health care to a person whose medical qualifications you had any reason to doubt, so also do not casually allow someone you know nothing about to enter the home when you are away to care for an elderly family member.

A word about our spiritual duties in relation to acting to prevent elderly abuse:

Friends, neighbours, and other relatives may be aware of the bullying and abuse…and yet not see fit to speak out. Maybe they feel it's none of their business, or that what happens in another household shouldn't concern them.

So they look the other way…turn a blind eye and pretend it doesn't concern them.

I want to assure them that it is everyone's business if another human being of advanced age is being bullied in their home.

We all have a responsibility to do what is right while on this earth. It is a moral imperative and a duty that comes with being human.

If you know that an elderly person is being abused…physically… mentally…or emotionally by their family, you have an absolute obligation to intervene.

This is part of your purpose for coming into this world…to stand at all times against injustice…to look out for your fellow human beings.

One day, you too will grow old…unless you quit the earth plane earlier…and then how will you feel if you have failed to take a stand on behalf of that victim of abuse and bullying all those years before.

As mentioned elsewhere in this book, we all have to account for our earth-life performance when we reach the end of the road on this earth.

Anyone who has abused a defenceless elderly person in the home… whether your own family or another human being entrusted to your care…will face justice in the Spirit World.

Again, though not "Hell" in the traditional or popular sense, the fate that awaits such transgressors in the Afterlife will be rigorous and comprehensive. He or she will have to be cleansed of that evil…that callous infliction of suffering on decent people who only asked to be treated with common humanity.

If you have subjected any man or woman to sadism or neglect or any form of ill-treatment, you will have to account for that despicable CRIME some day.

Elderly patients residing in nursing homes and sheltered housing also have a basic human *right* to expect fair treatment. They have reached the autumn or winter of their lives after punching in decades of earning a living, of experiencing all the manifold ups and downs of human existence.

Surely, they are entitled to be able to sit back and enjoy what time remains to them on earth in peace and security, free from the threat of abuse or the fear of what the nurse or carer might do or say to them next? We need to face up to the grim and revolting truth about what has happened, and is still happening, to elderly people.

Media exposes and Garda investigations have in recent times shone a spotlight on widespread physical, psychological, emotional, financial and sexual abuse.

People entrusted with the sensitive demanding task of caring for older people who have become incapacitated are generally decent, well-trained individuals of the highest integrity who provide an excellent service.

Unfortunately, a substantial minority of carers behave in a manner that is at variance with the requirements of their profession: They act in a way that is the exact opposite of caring…they *hurt* the people entrusted to their care, turning their frail lives into a hell of misery that no human being deserves.

The problem with "twilight abuse", as this crime is dubbed in medical circles, is that it very often goes unreported or unseen.

In many cases, the only people aware of it are the victim and the abuser. In circumstances where the victim is suffering from dementia, Alzheimer's, or any form of mild or serious mental illness, the abuse may never come to light, or even if the victim reports it, he or she may not be believed.

Increasing numbers of nursing homes have come under scrutiny over the past decade for alleged neglect and ill-treatment of residents.

Despite the public outcries and calls for more "whistle-blowing" to expose this crime, nursing home residents are still at the mercy of people who should never have become carers in the first place.

There are some situations, of course, in which neglect is not deliberate or malicious. The problem may stem from the deployment of under-qualified, under-trained, or overworked staff in the nursing home.

I appeal to anyone out there who has a relative in a nursing home or other private or publicly run professional care environment to be **one hundred percent certain** that their loved ones are being properly looked after.

One way you can do this…discreetly… is by visiting and seeing them without any of the staff present. You can then enquire as to how the patient or resident is being treated. You might also look for any signs or evidence of abuse if your relative hints that this is happening.

Some of the signs may be visible, such as bruises, black eyes, broken eye-glasses, or cuts resulting from assault or rough handling, or welts, bed sores, burns, weight loss, sprains, unreasonable methods or periods of restraint, and untreated medical ailments that would indicate neglect.

Other signs of ill-treatment or neglect may not be immediately apparent to you, such as broken bones, fractures, malnourishment, dehydration, and over-doses of medication.

You also need to look out for unusual or abrupt behavioural changes in the person you are concerned about, and it goes without saying you have cause to be suspicious if you are denied an opportunity to speak to the person alone in the absence of the carer or staff member.

Psychological and emotional abuse are not as easy to detect, so you have to be more vigilant.

Broach the subject gently, or in an indirect manner. What you are seeking is any definite indication that your loved one has been subjected to threats of any kind…humiliation, verbal abuse, unwarranted or prolonged isolation, or to emotional suffering whether this is deliberate or a side effect of neglect.

There are some signs to watch out for, including depression or a tendency to withdraw from day-to-day activities, adopting an uncommon silence.

If the person is normally upbeat and good humoured, and then you find that over a few visits he or she is "down" and devoid of motivation, it would be advisable to enquire as to the cause of this apparent mood change.

Unexpected and seemingly unexplained outbursts of anger on the part of the person also point to his or her having been bullied or otherwise ill-treated.

There is another form of abuse to which the elderly are equally vulnerable. That is the misuse or virtual theft of their financial resources. There are unscrupulous people who exploit an elderly person's dependency to swindle them out of funds, property or other assets.

This can happen with hard cash quite easily, but a more serious form of financial abuse is accomplished by means of forging signatures on cheques or cashing these without their permission or knowledge.

Signs to look out for in this instance are any unusual or unexplained changes in the person's normal banking habits or procedures.

Watch for any unauthorised withdrawals of money, whether by the ATM method or otherwise, unexplained changes in wills, an accumulation of bills that ought to have been paid but remain even though there should be adequate funds to pay these, and any noticeable siphoning away of possessions or funds that the person doesn't know about.

Bear in mind… if you are young or middle-aged, that you may one day be in the same vulnerable position as that elderly relative or friend that is in residential care right now.

When that time comes, you will want to be looked after and be protected from any abuse of your basic human rights.

So please…take immediate and decisive action if you suspect that a senior citizen may be a victim of abuse, whether in a family scenario or nursing home or any care situation.

Remember, that could be **you** one day!

☙

17

On the Threshold of the Afterlife…

You may have read of so-called Near Death Experiences. These provide people still living on earth with a brief but magnificent and memorable glimpse of what awaits them after death.

What happens is that the spirit hovers between the two worlds…as the physical body is either close to death or indeed has been declared clinically dead because the heart has stopped or the brain has ceased to function.

But in the typical NDE, the person who has temporally "died" to the earth plane is deemed not to have completed his life mission or allotted earthly term.

He must therefore return to his physical body to complete his assignment and learn whatever lessons remain to be learned before he finally reaches the point where he is prepared to leave behind his earth life and cross over to the Spirit World.

I would like to share with you my own personal Near Death Experience. Thirty-five years ago two of my children died during birth. In the first situation, I was close to death and the doctor indicated to me that I was dying.

I heard him saying, through a haze of pain and illness, that he and his colleagues were doing everything in their power to save me. Then suddenly the pain ceased…a feeling of absolute peace descended on me and I became weightless.

I found myself floating above the hospital bed, and could see the medical team beneath me, fighting desperately to save my life. There was a priest there too, probably administering the Last Rites. I saw other beds and the patients reclining in these.

For a moment or two, I wondered who that person was in the bed below me…then it dawned. That was *me* down there, or to be more precise my mortal body. The next thing that happened is that my brother, who had been murdered in England a few months before, appeared beside me.

He looked calm and radiant, a figure of peace and light. He spoke. He said: "Moira, you must return…you have children to rear…" I was excited by his appearance, especially after the dreadful death he had suffered.

He assured me that he was fine, and that everything was okay for him in his new home and state of being. I took his advice, and returned to my physical body. It was so tempting to go forward towards the light and exit this world of pain and sorrow.

But I had to complete my earth mission and care for my children and future grandchildren. Awaking in the hospital bed, I made a recovery and had to endure the discomfort of being back once again in the world of flesh and blood and suffering.

Two years later, I lost another child. Again, I was dying, according to the doctors and nurses in the hospital. This time, I was surround by a light…not the kind of illumination we are familiar with on earth or that one associates with bulbs or sunshine.

It was a deeply calming spiritual light that seemed to bathe my surroundings and envelop me in its ambience. Present within this radiance were people, some of whom

I recognised and others that were unknown to me.

They were loved ones…family members who had passed over. These approached me and I felt a surge of great love and support from them.

These spirit people, it seemed, were there to welcome me to the Other Side. I heard beautiful music of a kind that cannot be imagined or described in terms that would make any sense to a mind bound by earthly restrictions.

The Spirit World seemed to beckon me, and I had an overwhelming desire to join those radiant beings of light and love that awaited me.

But that was not to be…not yet. Again, my brother appeared. Calmly, and with a smile: "It's not your time…you must go back", he intoned. I felt so much at peace. I just wanted to quit my earth body and step across the Great Divide into the Spirit World.

But I realised and accepted that my appointed time had not arrived. The joys of the afterlife would be mine at a future date. But I had many assignments to complete first on the earth plane…a family to care for…and a lengthy career as a psychic medium, work that would bring hope, help, and consolation to thousands of people.

The Significance of Near Death Experiences

While there have been reports of near death experiences throughout the ages, there has been an upsurge in such reports in recent years. One reason for this is a greater preparedness to speak about having undergone this encounter with the divine.

Many of the barriers created by both atheistic science and intolerant religion have weakened, allowing people to be more open about psychic or spiritual happenings in their lives.

Another reason for the greater prevalence of NDE reports nowadays is the advanced nature of modern medical life-saving techniques.

Thus, someone who in the past would have died from a particular illness or disease or accident can today very often be "pulled back from the brink" of physical death with the aid of the latest medical technology.

From the 1970s in particular, increasing numbers of hospital patients have publicly spoken of their NDEs. From every part of the world come stories of people who were declared clinically dead by the doctors…but then seemingly came back to life or rallied unexpectedly.

Many of these people have described scenes similar to those I witnessed when I literally lived through and survived my own two brushes with death.

Though some details might vary in the different accounts, common features emerge. If you have read about Near Death situations, you will be familiar with these elements of the experience that almost everyone who has been through it has recalled:

Firstly, the sense of separation from the physical body, of being a spirit or independent being not as utterly dependent on that body you have just vacated as you may have felt throughout your material existence.

You gain a different perspective on life…knowing that the mind is far more important than the body and that consciousness can exist independently of it. For many, that is an earth-shattering, life-changing realisation.

Secondly, a feeling that something of great significance has occurred: You realise that though you are literally out of your mortal body you still feel as alive as before, maybe more so, and certainly more acutely aware of your surroundings than you would be while occupying that reclining image of yourself down on that bed, on the street, or wherever your earthly body happens to be lying.

Thirdly, you are likely to perceive loved ones who passed over before you. They are there to re-assure you that there is nothing to fear…if *they* have survived death and are now there to welcome you, what have you to worry about?

The fourth likely element in the Near Death Experience will be the encounter with a spiritual being who will advise you that your time for departure from the earth plane has not yet come.

In my case, it was as I mentioned my brother who appeared to relay that vital message to me. But other people have recalled a "being of radiant light", or a robed figure, or a Godlike entity manifesting to counsel them on that crucial issue.

Many recount a sensation, now made famous in movies and novels, of hurtling through a tunnel and arriving at the other end only to be told by a being of great compassion and divinity, to go back.

They may be granted an instantaneous "life-review" in which they see their entire earth life played back for them. This has a lasting impact on anyone who undergoes the process, often prompting a sincere, heartfelt resolution to "turn over a new leaf".

Another variant of the experience is that of arriving at a golden bridge, shimmering with light. The person may walk halfway across this bridge that joins the two worlds, the world of spirit and the material world, but is gently requested not to cross to the Other Side…not just yet.

There is more work to be done on earth, further lessons to be learned. Before turning back, he or she may be granted a glimpse, however fleeting, of what lies on the other side of that Rainbow Bridge. It is beautiful beyond words or earthly conception.

Seeing this, they have a profound longing to cross over, to sever their ties with that mortal body back down there in the hospital, on a battlefield, in an alleyway, or wherever, and move "towards the light".

But no. They must return. In the same way that suicide victims, or those who attempt suicide, are advised against ending one's life before the appointed time, so also are all of us counselled that we must complete our allotted span here on earth before we make that happy transition to our true home in the Spirit World.

Our day of departure will come soon enough. In the meantime, we must attend to our duties and responsibilities down here. Once we have "fought the good fight" and done our best to fulfil our mission here on earth, we can then happily, and with a clear conscience, rejoin our loved ones in that "Land Beyond the Stars".

☙❧

Listen...

Listen, can you hear me?
Listen, are you there?
It's very, very quiet here...
Are you anywhere out there?

Put your arms around me,
Hold me when I cry...
With your beautiful wings God gave you
Wipe these tears from my eyes.

Watch me while I'm sleeping...
Keep me safe at Day.
I know you're always with me.
You're never far away.

Andrea Bonny

18

A description of life on the Other Side …by a contented resident.

Readers will enjoy the following excerpt from the famed Woods/Greene collection of "direct voice" recordings with English medium Leslie Flint.

Mr. Flint specialised in the very rare form of mediumship called "direct voice" whereby spirits use a temporary voice box composed of ectoplasm to speak directly to people at a séance.

Mr. Flint and others who practise this method do not themselves speak for the duration of the séance, remaining silent. The voices come from various parts of the room. Mr. Flint's mediumship was tested rigorously and repeatedly during his lifetime and he passed every test with flying colours.

At a séance held in November 1967, a Mr. Ohlson came through, addressing those present, which included psychic researchers George Woods and Betty Greene.

Mr. Ohlson had been a personal friend of Betty Green and George Woods.

In his earth life, he had been intensely interested in spiritualism and the benefits of healing. George and Betty had arranged to record the séance.

Two separate pieces were recorded, and in each Mr. Ohlson's voice was clearly identifiable. The first recorded piece, which has the voice of the communicating spirit, Mr. Ohlson and those of Ms. Greene and Mr. Woods who converse with him, is quite brief and as follows:

Betty Greene: Hello: Who's that?

Spirit: Good Lord; Ohlson here!

George Woods: Oh, Mr. Ohlson

B.G: Hello, Mr. Ohlson

Mr. O.: How are you both?

G.W.: Oh, very well.

B.G.: Fine, thank you.

G.W.: And how are you getting on?

Mr. O.: Very well, no regrets, I'm very happy, I wouldn't come back if you

offered me all the gold in China. I'm perfectly well, and perfectly happy, and I can't tell you how marvellous it is to be dead!

G.W.: Well, I never!

The second recorded excerpt is much longer and contains fascinating insights into what the Spirit World looks like, confirming indeed what all genuine mediums have discovered in their work:

Mr. Ohlson: I've never known - well, you know I was very interested in all this and I

used to go to meetings -

Betty Greene: I've sat with you in this room -

Mr. O.: I know, that's a few years ago! My goodness me, people should think themselves lucky the day they kick the bucket!

B.G: What sort of condition did you find yourself in? What sort of place?

Mr. O: Well, as far as I'm concerned the place in which I found myself was, the nearest one can say is like some country place, it could be anywhere in a sense.

I mean there were trees and the birds, and just as if one was waking up in a country village, I realised that very soon afterwards - thousands and thousands of people.

Many, many live in what you'd call apartment houses - vast buildings housing thousands of people - all sounds rather like a large council estate, but nothing like that really.

I think this place I first came to, was a kind of reception station… it's the

only way I can put it - because it is pretty obvious that quite a lot of people when they first come, they do need help and attention, they need to be sort of helped through - it is a difficult period.

They don't take to it in the beginning, the realisation that they're separated from people they're close to and fond of on earth, when they realise that, although they can return, though very seldom do, they have the opportunity to have a chat or to comfort people they know and love on earth, they soon begin to realise that they are not acknowledged, and not welcomed.

Of course that's a great distress to people at first. That's why they do have these reception stations where there are advanced souls in attendance who know how to deal with these difficult cases, and in consequence they're soon nurtured into a new way of thinking. I think the most difficult cases are those who have strong convictions, religious convictions, narrow outlook.

Oh, we have community centres, and the children of course are one of the greatest joys. I've seen so many children who live with their people over here.

Of course many of them - their parents are still on earth, but they're taken in charge by people related to them like a grandmother and so on, but if there is no close tie or relationship there are always souls here who'll take charge.

And we have schools for them, and they learn all sorts of things, many of them more important than they learned at school on earth.

Do you know that there are vast cities here, but also you do get communities of peoples who because of nationality when on earth, and possibly because of their colour even, they have this habit of clinging together, or being together. This is usually, of course, a temporary thing with most of them.

We have great halls of learning, and of music. One can study any particular thing that appeals to one, mostly of an artistic endeavour, because it seems to me, I can realise that much more now, that art and the things of the mind and of the spirit are the things that are the most lasting obviously.

You see, this is a real world, but it's not a material world. Therefore we don't have the material aspects like you do on earth. You don't get vast factories for instance.

You don't get railways and stations, and thank God, you don't get all the noise, the filth and the dirt. Here it is a world of absolute beauty, and

there's the joy of progress in everything, the feeling of elation that comes with the realisation that all the time you're stepping forward.

There's always something new, something more interesting, some new experience, some new place to go to, new people to visit, fresh arrivals coming over from the earth. People we have known and loved, helping them to settle, getting them interested in all sorts of things over here.

It's not a wishy-washy affair over here. It's not some sort of vague something.

It's a real existence, and we are in our own way as physical as you are. Yet *it's not a physical body as you have it.*

To all outward appearance it may look the same, but it isn't, the construction is different. I mean we are living on a vibration that is so far removed from earth, and everything is rarefied in consequence and everything that we do has a meaning and purpose.

Your world to me seems - well, it is as if there's a dark, dreary foggy

atmosphere. Of course the thought forces emanating from your world en masse are so terrible. There's all this upset, hatred, bitterness and malice. I wouldn't want to come back to it.

This is a transmission of my thought via this artificial vocal voice box, call it what you will, which transmits it into sound. It is artificially created because after all we can speak over here - we can communicate if we wish by the vocal effort - we learn very quickly that the best form of communication is a mental process.

This is a world of mental reality, which by the very power that generates it, creates, what you might call, a physical condition or picturisation of things.

The more one sort of develops mentally and spiritually here, the more conscious and aware you become of other places, vistas and people. It's just a matter of tapping the source and becoming, as it were, tuned into it.

Betty Greene: Mr. Ohlson, how do you spend your time now?

Mr. Ohlson: Time, time, time! Well, we're not conscious of time. Time does not mean anything to us. By coming back to you we're conscious of time to some extent.

People say 'Oh well, I'm sure so-and-so will come and speak because it's his birthday.' Well, we couldn't care less in a sense about birthdays.

In fact we probably wouldn't even remember it was our birthday if it were not for the fact that we pick up the idea or the thought from the consciousness of the individual *near and dear to us on earth.*

End of Excerpt

George and Betty conversed further with their old friend. The séance concluded after about half an hour. The two researchers recorded hundreds of other "direct voice" séances, all of which offer very strong evidence of the existence that every medium knows to await us after death.

Many of these recordings can be accessed on the Internet and you can listen to them…to the voices of those who, though dead to this earth plane, continue to live wholesome and happy lives in the Spirit World.

☙

19

Once Upon a Time in Ireland…

Among the many people who call to me for readings are women who gave up their babies for adoption at birth…and have been regretting this decision ever since. Conversely, men and women who *were* those babies also tell me their stories.

Both parents and children in these situations have a harrowing tale to relate of abandonment, shame, guilt, rejection, bitterness, and misunderstanding.

Whatever reason a mother has for parting with her natural child, it is inevitable that she will suffer from feelings of guilt and anxiety, perhaps for the remainder of her life, because of that crucial occurrence.

She may go on to have other children that become her acknowledged family, and indeed this may well be a perfectly contented and reasonably happy familial experience for her and her offspring.

The marriage, if there is one, may also be a loving, fulfilling relationship. But there will always be that nagging thought…that persistent question: Where is that dear child I gave birth to all those years ago? What has become of him or her…how is that lost one…my own flesh and blood, faring in the world…and wouldn't it be marvellous to see them once again? Even once.

As for the child: He or she grows to maturity and begins to ask questions too…different ones, like: who *was* or *is* this woman…my real mother, and why did she give me away like that? How could any mother do such a thing, they ask themselves, and maybe others also to whom they confide their heartache and sense of incompleteness.

Curiosity and feelings of abandonment may give way to a determination to track down this mother they have never known. Some such people will devote years or decades to the search for their natural mother. If and when a meeting takes place, there can be mixed emotions.

The mother may be thrilled to see the long lost child, now an adult, and the former child may be ecstatic at the prospect of seeing this person who brought him or her into the world.

But other emotions are liable to surface too…bitter recriminations may follow the initial relief and happiness at being re-united. The questions and accusations may start pouring out…and the attempts at explaining that may or may not convince the son or daughter or assuage the deep-seated feelings of rejection or betrayal.

I advise anyone who has located a birth mother in this way to please show some understanding…be patient…listen carefully to the story of what *motivated* that other human being who gave birth to you.

Listen to her account of the circumstances that prevailed in *that other time and other place*. Do not reject her.

It has been said by a great poet that "the past is another country". Consider for a moment just how *different* that past has been from the society that has evolved out of it. Consider why many Irish women had to part with their beloved babies.

Let me tell you of another time and a different Ireland of which none of us can be proud.

Fairy tales begin with the words "Once upon a Time", but this is no fairy tale. It is a true story that could have come straight out of a living nightmare.

Not so long ago, in the first three-quarters of the twentieth century, any Irish woman who found herself pregnant was liable to be sent to what she was told was "a special place to do penance". These were purpose-built and impeccably designed punishment centres, known as the Magdalene Asylums.

Most of the centres were run by the various Catholic Church orders. More than 30,000 women were incarcerated in the Asylums at one time or another.

People today may not grasp the enormity of the crime that society and the religious orders perpetrated against these women, who were completely innocent of any criminal offence or civil misdemeanour.

They were banished to virtual slavery and torment for being *single mothers!*

Their *families*, out of shame and to avoid the harsh and unrelenting criticism of the clergy, had them signed into these horrid places.

Women confined in the centres were expected to do daily penance and work long hours, especially in the laundries. The Magdalene homes resembled prisons in some respects: the confinement against one's will, the strict rules regarding behaviour, and the lack of civil rights that applied to people outside the institutions.

But they were *worse* than prisons. The religious supervisors in charge of the "fallen women" enforced discipline in ways that even prison managements would not tolerate: The women were *flogged and beaten daily* for the slightest breach of the rules.

They were mocked and jeered and called hurtful names in front of other inmates by the supervisors… in the showers or while working.

They were beaten for having "impure thoughts", for looking the wrong way at a superior, for swearing, for breaking a rule of silence at certain hours of the day or night, or for neglecting to say their prayers on time.

Superiors also picked on inmates just to bully them or because they felt like picking on them.

Any excuse and a woman could be severely chastised. They only got to leave the institution on rare occasions, such as the annual Corpus Christi Procession when they would be dressed up in specially designed "sin bin outfits" denoting their Magdalene status.

A photograph I include shows one such procession. Note the presence of a strong Garda escort to prevent any of the Magdalene women from escaping.

Every day, they had to listen to sermons and lectures reminding them of the terrible sin that had landed them in the institution…*having a baby without getting married first.*

Most traumatic of all, for some women, was what happened if the babies they had conceived out of wedlock happened to be born within the walls of the institution: The babies were snatched by the overseers and given up for adoption.

Throughout the first part of the twentieth century, right into the 1970s, these babies were separated from their mothers and in many cases SOLD to adoptive couples in America. Thus, thousands of single mothers around Ireland lost their babies to this cruel religious extremism.

Though often likened to prison, I think the Magdalene centres bore a stronger resemblance to the concentration camps of Nazi Germany.

For, just as the Nazis sent Gays and Lesbians to camps, single mothers were singled out and stigmatised in much the same way here in Ireland. And this was all done in the name of so-called "religion".

Yet the women were guilty of no crime. It was the people who set up those punishment centres and ran them that had a case to answer.

The full horror of the Magdalene era only came to light in 1993…and almost by accident. A religious order in Dublin was selling off a section of a convent for real estate.

When development work commenced on the site, the workers had to exhume the bodies of more than 150 women who had been buried in unmarked graves. It turned out they had been Magdalene inmates who had died while serving their sentences for giving birth outside marriage.

After exhumation, the bodies were cremated and re-interred in a mass grave on the orders of the people who had run the punishment centre.

In 1999, this event was made public, and an outcry followed, leading former inmates of this and other Magdalene homes to come forward and speak out about their ordeal.

News reports and television documentaries followed, exposing a litany of physical, sexual, emotional, and psychological abuse in the centres. **The last Magdalene home in Ireland was still operating in 1996.**

Though the centres have now all been consigned to history, the legacy of that terrible era continues to haunt our country. Many of the babies stolen from the women have grown up in other lands and with different parents.

Not all babies born "out of wedlock" back in those days were sold to Americans or given for adoption in this country. Many children ended up in one or other of the vast system of industrial schools and homes, again mainly run by religious orders.

Instead of being educated for adult life, these children were, like the Magdalenes, subjected to an almost daily regime of bullying and beatings. Many of them also suffered sexual abuse at the hands of their supposedly "holy" guardians.

Children, and teenagers, lived in constant fear of men and women in black who strutted about, wielding leather straps and bamboo canes, lashing out in all directions at the children.

And if any inmate escaped from one of these centres, the guards helped to track them down and return them…as if they were dangerous criminals. Severe punishment awaited any child or teenager who attempted escape.

As with the Magdalenes, it is only in recent years that the abuses these children suffered have come to light. Mass graves have been unearthed at various centres around the country.

It was found that children who died mysteriously while in these so-called industrial schools and homes were buried in shallow graves with no markers to indicate their place of burial.

Here are two selected excerpts from *Founded on Fear*, written by an inmate of Letterfrack Industrial School, Peter Tyrell. His experience was typical of what children had to endure in these centres. He never got to see his writings in print, because Peter committed suicide in 1968.

The book, comprising notes, extracts from diaries, and letters he wrote concerning his youth and childhood, was published almost four decades after his tragic death.

Excerpt One:

"…Brother Dooley beats the senior boys on the back and the legs with a walking stick. He beats John Cane so severely that he leaves the ranks and runs screaming out of the yard, he goes to the lavatory and refuses to leave. He is now being beaten for a long time, four boys are ordered to carry him to the infirmary. He is bleeding from the mouth and nose. John Cane is sixteen and due to leave the school very soon. We are marching around the square, and Brother Dooley rushes through the ranks and hits Scally with the stick on the back, for being out of step. We are now dismissed. That evening we are given a lecture lasting an hour, we then say the Rosary. Brother Dooley asks us all to pray for him as he is suffering from Rheumatism. The next morning I am awake early. Brother Walsh has just returned from the chapel, and he is taking six or seven lads away for being awake. It's now about 6 am. I can hear the children screaming. He has taken them to the

washroom and flogged them with a stick. It is a crime to be awake before we are called…"

Excerpt Two:

"…The centre was swept by a different person each day in turn. We then washed under our own tables, by soaking a cloth in water, and just wiping the floor which was tiled with red and white tiles. Then one boy from each table washed the centre of the floor twice a week or whenever Brother Vale told us. We scrubbed the floor on our hands and knees with a brush and soap and water. In this case all the tables had to be shifted to one end and then to the other. It was whilst this work was being done that we were severely beaten from behind. As we were in line on hands and knees, we were flogged on the backside with the rubber. We must continue to wash the floor and not stop or look up. If we did cry or scream we only get a few blows but on the other hand, if we showed any sign of fear the punishment would be very much greater, and should any boy jump up from the pain of the blows, it was just agony to watch the result. When the floor was all washed and scrubbed it would be examined, and very often the very same thing would be repeated all over again, and of course the same beating. It was awful to see the children trembling, their faces twitching, their faces were pale, drawn and haggard. Most of them were too terrified to cry…"

Survivors of this era speak of their days in the industrial schools in the same way that former inmates of the Nazi camps relate their ordeal. Understandably, because they were, and are, *victims of an enormous crime against humanity committed right here in Ireland.*

Some have had to receive life-long counselling and therapy to help them cope with the unendurable legacy of that experience. Others turned to drink and drugs and their lives were scarred completely by what happened to them.

The culprits at first denied any wrongdoing when confronted with their actions. They pointed out, in their defence, that society tolerated what they did, which was unfortunately true.

Because…make no mistake…many people knew what was happening

behind the grim grey walls of the institutions...and did nothing. They looked the other way. One wonders how "Christians", as they called themselves, could so easily have forgotten the words of Christ himself... when he castigated any abuse of children as a grave and terrible sin.

So spare a thought for "yesterday's children"...regardless of what age they are now.

And for the women who endured abuse and torture in those other institutions.

And for the babies they were forced to give up by those men and women in black who ruled with an iron fist.

And please...if you are the son or daughter of a woman who gave you up for adoption at birth...try to understand her motives, whatever they were.

Try to forgive and let healing commence.

Your feelings of abandonment and betrayal are understandable and perfectly human. But try to understand **why** she may have felt compelled to act the way she did, and that, just as you feel let down by her action, she too has suffered over all those years.

Bear in mind...as you consider your own plight and hers...that she had to live in a different society from the one *you* know and understand.

Remember what life was like for so many thousands of innocent women...*single mothers*...once upon a time in Ireland.

20

Psychic Attacks

As we progress through life, we have to be on our guard against people and situations that threaten us or have the potential to cause us harm.

We bolt our doors to keep out burglars, we take precautions to ensure our personal safety when we travel and in our dealings with strangers.

Yet we often overlook the hidden dangers that can hurt with equal or even greater severity. The power of thought, generated by people hostile to us for one reason or another, has the potential to inflict mental or sometimes physical suffering and we must take care to protect ourselves against this also.

If someone really hates you, or is jealous of you, that person can telepathically wreak havoc on your life via negative thought waves and the sheer force of his or her spiteful thought projections.

One way to counteract such attacks is to meditate and pray to the Higher Spirit. Ask for protection from all hostile or malevolent forces and remember that the power of love is always greater and more potent than the power of hatred and evil.

There are of course other forces, far more lethal and spiritually destructive that human beings have to contend with. Mediums, as I have explained in another chapter, have to protect themselves when entering the trance state from entities and energies of the darker kind.

We do this by invoking the guardianship of our spirit guides, to ward off all evil influences and distractions because, and this must always be borne in mind, the forces of good and evil in the Universe are locked in perpetual struggle for dominance…the dark and sinister elements forever striving to gain the upper hand.

I know mediums who have experienced psychic attacks in the course of their work. These can manifest in numerous forms. You can awaken from a trance with scratches on your body or bloodshot eyes, the result of dark entities or energies attempting to interfere with work that tends "towards the light".

Failure to protect yourself can leave you open to the forces of evil. If you saw the film *The Exorcist*, you will have some idea or mental image of the horrendous negative energies that assail humankind…and especially people striving to do God's work on this planet.

This battle between good and evil is never-ending, and has been raging largely unseen and unnoticed down through the centuries. For example, you have heard of witchcraft, and the two kinds of witches that have traditionally practised the hidden arts.

Since prehistoric times witches have tuned into higher forces, some to do good, others to seek power over people or to curse them. Witches and sorcerers have been a part of all cultures and the forces they invoked were- and **ARE**- very real.

Both the dark and white witches of the past were careful to protect themselves when performing their psychic activities or engaging in the occult rituals that conferred power on them.

One method was for the witches to draw a circle around themselves… invoking protection for all those within it.

The circle had a special symbolism. In addition to its protective purpose, it was deemed to be a connecting symbol between the earth world and the hidden world, enabling the witches to make contact with spirits and other discarnate entities.

The good or white witches are the ones who practise white magic… helping their fellow human beings in much the same way that honest mediums strive to bring hope and consolation to people who seek reassurance about life after death.

They perform wholesome rituals that summon forth the positive energies and their lifestyles reflect the life-affirming qualities of a decent and healthy approach to living.

They endeavour to cure illness or disease, make crops grow, or help people to find love and happiness. The dark witch however dabbles with malevolent energies and attaches himself or herself, deliberately or otherwise, to the force of evil in the universe that opposes the Light.

They use charms, effigies, and curses to hurt their enemies. Though spells might sound a bit harmless in today's material world, their potency is beyond dispute and if a witch casts a spell it can have an effect on the intended victim unless that person has shielded herself from such a calculated psychic attack.

The prevalence of white and dark witches can therefore be seen as part of the perpetual conflict between good and evil. And the forces invoked are as real as the ground under your feet or the air you breathe, as I know from many years of practising as a psychic medium.

I take care to protect myself when dealing with the higher dimensions and ethereal or spiritual energies. My guides and angels look after me and have never failed me when I call upon them.

But while I take special precautions to protect myself in all situations involving communication with the Spirit World or spiritual healing, there are times when, due to the sheer pressure and level of commitment to the process, one can overlook this necessity or let down one's guard.

One such occasion was in 2005, when I visited an international healing seminar in Germany hosted by the renowned spiritual healer *John of God* from Brazil. The event was staged in a large building and attracted huge crowds.

People of all ages and from walks of life had converged on the town to which this celebrated psychic had travelled to offer hope and healing.

Though many people benefited from the experience, and I was impressed by his abilities, the very size of the attendance created a problem: It meant that proper spiritual cleansing and psychic protection might be overlooked in the hectic overcrowded conditions and the intense pressure of the occasion.

There was a lot of pushing and shoving and jostling as people waited their turn to meet the healer.

This frantic conveyer-belt-like environment is not always conducive to the appropriate cleansing that is necessary in situations involving psychic energies and contact with the higher dimensions.

After my own encounter with *John Of God*, I went on my way like the others, content that I had got to meet him and receive healing.

But in the excitement and frenzied atmosphere, I overlooked the need to be spiritually protected from any dark or negative energies or mischievous entities that might be present.

Such presences in that situation would have been almost inevitable, because as I've mentioned the dark forces are *always* warring with the forces of the Light, just as black magic is in eternal opposition to white magic.

On my way out of the healing centre, I became aware of a ghostly or ethereal presence behind me. I looked around. I perceived a very tall male form, completely in black…and apparently growing larger by the second.

I said to my daughter Tina, who was with me: "there's a spirit but I don't know if he's a doctor or what". We kept walking on, and I noticed that this phantom materialization was still pursuing us.

When the hotel came into view he was still hovering behind us.

We entered the hotel and gave no serious thought for the time being to what I had seen. But then, later that day, we left the hotel to go shopping.

I will never forget what happened. I was linking my daughter, walking along the pavement…when suddenly and without any warning I was wrenched from her by a powerful force…levitated off the ground…and thrown across against the wall of the hotel.

I had become the victim of a psychic attack, and the energies involved were quite powerful. I suffered two fractures to my shoulder that caused me intense pain and discomfort.

My daughter and several passers-by witnessed this frightening incident. They gazed wide-eyed and disbelieving…stunned by what they had seen. Some of them rushed to my aid, enquiring what had happened to me.

This brush with the "dark side" that is forever present in our midst served as yet another reminder to me of just how essential it is to have protection from any form of psychic attack.

I would advise anyone who is developing his or her abilities as a medium or a psychic to take account of these dark forces and to *always* ensure that their spirit guides are there to safeguard them in their dealings with the supernatural.

☙

21

Have we met before?

> Into my heart an air that kills
> From yon far country blows:
> What are those blue remembered hills,
> What spires, what farms are those?

The verse from A.E. Housman's poem has often been associated with a belief in reincarnation.

This is another subject relevant to any consideration of what happens to the human entity after death.

Essentially it is the belief, well supported by evidence, that we incarnate not merely to live one life and then die, but that we return time after time from the Spirit World, which is our true home, to gain further experience of life on earth.

At birth, we descend to the earth world to commence a new life in a physical body…at death we cast off that restrictive body to enter once again the joyous realms of spirit and after a prolonged stay in the Spirit World, we may opt to incarnate and take on a new set of challenges in the earth world.

Actual belief in reincarnation has been very strong and widespread among the major religions of the Orient for centuries. Hinduism and Buddhism are the belief systems most closely identified with the concept of re-birth, but it has also been central to the religious beliefs of tribal societies in many parts of the world.

In the third century A.D. the renowned Egyptian philosopher Plotinus hailed reincarnation as "a doctrine recognised throughout antiquity… the soul expiates its sins and afterwards passes into new bodies, there to undergo new trials…"

In the 19th century the Theosophical Movement popularised the concept of reincarnation in the West and today, opinion polls conducted in America and Europe show that increasing numbers of people now accept that reincarnation is a fact.

A famed psychic and novelist, Joan Grant, claimed to have recalled thirty-one different previous lives. She wrote about these lives in books, the best known of which is *Far Memory*.

Though she presented the books as novels, Joan made it clear that she was drawing on her memories of past incarnations in all her historical writings. She appears to have had the rare gift known as "total recall" which enables a person to remember former lives on earth in great detail.

Most people do not recall their past life experiences because, according to psychic researchers, we generally forget who and what we did in those former times once we leave the Spirit World to begin yet another earth life.

Aside from its status as a well-known religious belief or concept, reincarnation is supported by compelling evidence, among the most important findings in its favour being those of the legendary Canadian doctor and psychic researcher, Professor Ian Stevenson.

He became involved in psychic research shortly after assuming a post as Professor of Psychiatry at the University of Virginia in 1957. He undertook a number of projects concerning survival of death and extra-sensory perception and then became interested in the concept of reincarnation.

He wondered if there was any real proof that human beings live more than one life on earth. In 1960, he published his acclaimed essay entitled: *"The Evidence for Survival from Claimed Memories of Former Incarnations"*.

In this, he drew attention to forty-four documented cases of past life recollection he had examined. Each of the people named had been able to recall previous lives. The identities had been thoroughly checked and proven to have been real people.

He then set off in search of further evidence of possible reincarnation cases. His travels took him to Brazil, Ceylon, India, Alaska, and Lebanon, among another countries. Children who described former lives had their claims checked in the course of his extensive research and investigation.

The alleged previous lives were followed up and investigated and people in the villages of localities where the children claimed to have lived before were interviewed to confirm or refute the claims.

In many cases, a child would have the same tastes in food as the person he or she claimed to have been in the former life, as well as a whole range of other minor likes and dislikes. Some had traces of scars on parts of their bodies corresponding to where they had been wounded or injured in previous incarnations.

Others had inherited musical talents or other specific abilities from their past earth life bodies. And there were those who spoke in languages unfamiliar to them in their conscious state when hypnotised.

Dr. Stevenson found that birthmarks could be traced back to past lives also. He discovered that an Alaskan fisherman, shortly before dying, had promised that two prominent moles on his body would appear in the body he occupied in his next life on earth. Nine months after he died, his daughter in law had a baby…with the identical moles on its body

By the middle of the 1990s, the professor had more than 2,500 such cases on his files...all of them providing compelling evidence that we do indeed reincarnate.

One of the most celebrated reincarnation cases was that of Shanti Devi in India. When four years old, the girl claimed to have lived another life in the town of Mutta, a hundred miles from her own village.

She gave graphic descriptions of the town and of people who lived in it, though she had apparently never been there. Bemusement on the part of her parents turned to astonishment when she named the man who was her husband in that former life!

The parents arranged for the man to call to their home, if only to clear up the mystery and maybe put an end to their daughter's persistent ramblings. The moment he entered their house, Shanti recognised him immediately and revealed a secret known only to him and herself... namely that she had buried one hundred rupees in a room of her husband's house. He confirmed that this was true.

The parents then took Shanti to Mutta, alleged native town of her former life, and she again surprised them by recognising many people and landmarks in that locality.

So-called child prodigies also point to past lives. The great Austrian composer Mozart, for example, was playing and composing music from a very early age and the world is teeming with people whose talent in many fields manifested in childhood...before they had an opportunity to receive any special guidance or tuition that would account for their special "gift".

It is in dreams, as mentioned earlier, that many of us may recall snatches of a previous life. If you have strong nocturnal images of unfamiliar surroundings of a bygone age, or of wearing clothes of another time and place, this may well be a past life memory.

Hypnotic regression has greatly facilitated research into this fascinating subject. Hypnotherapists, who can regress people through hypnosis to the earliest years of their lives, have experimented with taking some volunteers back further...to before they were born into the world to commence their present existence in physical bodies.

Under hypnosis, they casually speak in different languages; describe locations and situations from centuries back. Increasing numbers of people nowadays are opting to be "regressed" to learn more about their past incarnations.

Apart from its curiosity value, this can be valuable in some cases, especially if a person suffers from a phobia such as fear of heights, or open spaces, or of confinement for example. A person who has an obsessive fear of confinement may have died in conditions of confinement at the end of a past life.

Likewise, there have been cases of regression where people with unexplained pains and aches discovered under hypnosis that they had been wounded in the affected parts of the body in previous lives.

One of the most influential of the hypnotherapists who have devoted themselves to regressing people to former lives has been California-based Michael Newton. In addition to enabling subjects to recall past life experiences, he has gone an important step further and explored what happens *between earth lives*...in the Spirit World.

His work, as recounted in his excellent book *Journey of Souls*, vindicates the experience and knowledge of mediums like myself in relation to the nature of the Spirit World, what happens to each of us when we get there after death, and the kind of reception that awaits us on the Other Side.

He was able to establish through his thousands of past life regressions, and regressions to life in the Spirit World; how we choose another physical body when we decide to come back to earth again, how we meet up with our soul mates, and how each person is judged fairly and in accordance with his or her behaviour and achievements upon returning to the Spirit World after death.

Dr. Newton's work is most welcome because it demonstrates the true value and significance of mediumship.

A question people ask about reincarnation is how much time (earth time that is) elapses between the death of one's mortal body and the spirit's re-entry onto the earth world. The answer is that this varies widely.

From all the research undertaken on reincarnation and hypnotic regression it is clear that people who arrive in the Spirit World *before* their appointed time will, as a rule, reincarnate far sooner than someone who has led a long life on earth.

Mediums have found in their work that there are advanced souls who have been in the Spirit World for centuries of earth time without reincarnating. These might include the great scientists, philosophers, artists, composers, doctors, and healers who are continuing their life-enhancing missions from the Other Side, helping human beings in a variety of ways, such as by inspiring or aiding us as Spirit Guides.

It must be remembered that the earth plane is a School of life and that souls that have learned all the lessons this world has to teach may opt to remain on the higher levels, or, if they choose to incarnate again, they will do so not to learn…but to pass on their great knowledge and help people who have not yet reached their level of spiritual advancement.

Thus, for example, spiritual giants like Christ, the Buddha, Krishna etc did not come to earth simply to learn the hard lessons like most humans have to, but to assist humanity in its spiritual evolution…to in effect help the rest of us to become better people!

You might ask… If reincarnation is a fact, how could the great Christian churches have overlooked it…and why did Christ not seem to mention it?

Unfortunately, the early Christian Church was only too well aware of this concept, but felt threatened by it. And of course many of the original teachings of Christ were diluted or altered by the Church founders.

A Church Council that convened in the year 553 forbade any discussion of reincarnation by Christians, effectively silencing any of its members who accepted the belief from openly "declaring" for it.

This draconian measure led to almost fourteen centuries of reincarnation as a belief being consigned to the wilderness of forbidden faiths within Christendom.

This was a tragedy, because it robbed Christians of this "missing link" in their own belief system.

They accepted that the human spirit survived physical death and continued to exist in another state…but they failed to take into account that in addition to crossing over to the Spirit World at death, *we also return periodically from that exalted state to live again here on earth in flesh and blood bodies.*

Yet, one of the most distinguished and influential of the early Christian Church's own theologians, Origen, preached that the soul **pre-existed** in past earth lives and returned to earth to live again.

And the Gnostics, who had a major influence on Christianity in its early stages, had a strong belief in reincarnation.

To these profoundly spiritual people, who meditated and prayed and fasted as part of their religious routine, the idea that we live many earth lives was not only a logical belief…but one supported by evidence similar to that which Professor Stevenson would provide centuries later…some of them could recall their own previous lives.

Gnostic derives from the Greek word meaning Knowledge, and these spiritually evolved people were far advanced in their grasp of the greater realities of life and death.

They paid the price of their courage and wisdom when they suffered persecution by the religious authorities across Europe due to their refusal to accept some of the key beliefs of the Official Church.

Linked to the concept of reincarnation is the Law of Karma. This is just a word used to denote the universal law of cause and effect that rules human existence and behaviour on this earth.

What it means is that whatever you do…no matter what action, good or bad, you undertake…it will have an effect. And you, at some point in time, will experience the positive or negative "boomerang effect" of all your actions.

As I explained elsewhere in this book, nobody can escape the consequences of his behaviour, regardless of how clever or devious or cunning he may think himself in the short term, or whatever the outcome of legal proceedings.

If you take a life in an act of murder, you may not experience the Karmic "kick-back" from that terrible act immediately…perhaps not for several years, or maybe not even within the span of your present earth life.

But at some point…the consequences of that act will be staring you in the face and you will have to re-pay that heavy Karmic debt you have incurred by prematurely ending the life of a fellow human being.

Conversely, your every *good deed* also has consequences…positive ones…for you.

So strive to do good whenever and wherever you can. People who form very close relationships in one lifetime are likely, according to psychic researchers, to meet up again in future incarnations.

If the relationship was rooted in love, this will carry through into the next earth life, and if it was one of enmity or negative dealings, the people concerned will have to sort out those difficulties.

If a person incurs a particular obligation to another human being, that obligation has to be paid…if not in the present life, then in a future incarnation. It is common, the researchers say, for members of a family to have been in the same family in past lives…but with different life assignments and challenges.

For example, the person who is your brother this time around may have been your sister, mother, or father last time. Or the man or woman who is giving you a difficult time at work may have been someone you wronged in some way in a previous life.

As explained in the chapter on Gays, Lesbians, and Transsexuals, men with deep-seated feminine qualities or characteristics and women with pronounced male characteristics or tendencies in the majority of cases tend to be people who have incarnated in the wrong bodies, whether inadvertently or by design.

They deserve our respect and understanding because they are in no way abnormal or guilty of any offence whatsoever.

In life, every smile counts. Every kind word. Every kind thought. Every act that eases the pain of humanity in even the smallest degree. None of us is perfect, and life is full of friction, misunderstanding, and conflict.

People fall out. Rows are part of life. Relationships flounder. But we must strive to ensure that our credit outweighs the Karmic debts incurred by humanity's dark side.

Much is written and spoken nowadays about reducing our "carbon footprint" as we progress through life, a reference to the need to be more environmentally friendly, avoid pollution etc.

But far more important is our "spiritual footprint"…the overall effect each of our lives has on the physical and spiritual wellbeing of our fellow human beings. Just as rivers, lakes, and the countryside are at the mercy of polluters…evil thoughts and actions pollute the psychic atmosphere of our planet.

We need to counteract the negative and destructive forces with kindness, positive interventions, and compassion. The notion that *What Goes Around Comes Around* does not have to be bad news…or a forbidding proverb.

We are the masters of our own destiny. We have the free will to choose between the light and the darkness. If we do good and shun evil, we have nothing to fear from what eventually "comes around" in the great Circle of Life…whenever or wherever it arrives to greet us!

❧

22

After Death…a World Worth Waiting for!

Whilst it would require the pages of a thousand books to even attempt describing the wonderful world of spirit that awaits all of us, I will offer here for the benefit of my readers an account based on the evidence, knowledge, and psychic perceptions of mediums down through the ages.

It is remarkable how their accounts and perceptions of the Spirit World are consistent with each other, each lending support to the accumulated wisdom of mankind concerning the next phase of our soul's great journey towards God.

Regardless of the cause of death, or the duration of the dying process, or of what pain or anxiety may have preceded the final moment of departure from the physical body, we are assured that **all fear and worry and pain disappear once death takes place**…melting away like snow before warm rays of sunshine.

The dying itself may have featured the calming influence of loved ones from the Spirit World gathering at the bedside…or making themselves known or seen to the dying person…a reassuring presence and a promise of the better life that is about to begin.

As in the Near Death Experiences discussed elsewhere in this book, these deathbed apparitions may include actual travel to the spiritual realms…where the person is granted a glimpse of Heaven.

He or she may briefly return to the physical body following this vision or experience, contented and free from fear, before finally crossing over.

Upon arrival in the Spirit World, each newcomer is made to feel welcome and very much at home by loved ones and guides.

Shortly thereafter…though there is no "time limit" because earthly time has ceased to have meaning once we cross over…we have to undergo the Life Review that so many psychics and mediums, as well as Near Death subjects have spoken or written about.

This involves re-visiting the earth life that has just ended. It is not like a court sitting in judgement. It is a cleansing process, wherein we have to account for every action and every thought from that lifetime, and we are shown how all our thoughts and actions affected other people.

We see and feel and hear and otherwise experience **WITH GREAT INTENSITY** the effects of our own lives on each and every person we had dealings with, or who were influenced, or impacted on, for good or ill, by our behaviour.

Having experienced the life review, we have ample opportunity to reflect on our progress in the life just lived, and how we might improve on that performance if and when we decide to re-incarnate to commence another gruelling series of lessons in the School of Life that is the earth plane!

Serious offenders are more likely to re-incarnate sooner than those people who have led reasonably decent lives, because they feel impelled, usually, to atone for their evil ways and get "back on track".

One must be careful about judging even the most heinous wrongdoer or social malcontent…because at some point in the past we too may have done wrong, and indeed may now be paying the price for it!

When people speak of "moving towards the light" in Near Death Experiences or actual death or psychic visions, what they are attempting to describe is far brighter and more beautiful than any source of illumination, even the sun in the sky, familiar to humans on the earth plane.

It is not an energy produced by fire or gas or electricity or anything common to the world of matter. It is a spiritual light that radiates compassion and the unconditional love of the Higher Spirit.

And the Spirit World is not illuminated by any artificial source of light such as we know on earth. All is light and tranquillity, though in the lower levels where murderers, spousal abusers, and other serious offenders dwell there are shades of darkness and a murky atmosphere conducive to their negative thoughts and actions.

Apart from obvious crimes of great magnitude, there is a particular human emotion that may land you in the lower levels if you surrender to it in life. That is **jealousy**, the most destructive of all the emotions that we need to curb and control in our dealings with other people.

It wrecks families and poisons human relationships. In romantic or sexual matters it is especially lethal, with people yielding to feelings of spite to hurt others whose success in love they envy but cannot have.

Jealousy is a bitter and horrible attitude of mind that we must control and if possible eliminate altogether from our lives. In the lower regions of the afterlife, jealous people congregate and feed off each other's spite and nastiness. They are the ones depicted in ancient paintings and drawings of evil spirits.

While they may not be completely evil, they are certainly in need of cleansing because jealousy has **no place** in a world free of such lowly and poisonous behaviour.

Only when they have purged themselves of their envy and covetousness can they attain to the higher levels of the Spirit World.

One of the first big changes that people notice when they enter the Spirit World after death is the far greater range of colours…on earth we perceive only a small number of the vast multiplicity of colours and hues that fill the universe.

The higher one progresses through the Spirit World, the brighter and more beautiful is that range and variety of colour, and the more energised.

Needless to say, artists in particular are truly "at home" with this welcome change from the earth plane, where by comparison we live in a shadowy and lacklustre world.

And each colour has its own spiritual force. On earth, we often remark on how a colour affects our mood, or how some colours clash. That awareness of colour psychology is greatly magnified in the Spirit World...with each colour eliciting its own unique response or feeling from you.

But absent is the downside familiar to us humans on the earth plane, for all the colours of the Next Life are in harmony, reflecting the truth and transcendent beauty of a place...or state of being...that is well worth looking forward to!

Likewise with sound. This has a positively divine quality in the Spirit Realms, with different frequencies unknown and unimaginable to humans confined by five sensory earthly faculties.

This is why composers have far greater latitude to continue their creative work in the Spirit World, as they are no longer confined or restricted by the rules of the physical plane.

It is also one of the reasons why people who hear "spirit melodies" whole meditating or in a trance state or undergoing a Near Death experience rhapsodise about the "heavenly" music they heard...like nothing they have ever heard or dreamt of.

You may have been "transported" in life by a gifted musician or singer performing at his or her best...but just wait till you hear the Voices of Angels...and the great choirs of Heaven!

Are you worried about lack of speech training, or dumbness? Stop worrying, because in the Spirit World you can communicate by thought, and do so comfortably with any of the other inhabitants…language being only a convention of the earth plane that enables us to make ourselves understood to each other.

But on the higher levels you have no need of words or language…unless you wish to communicate in that fashion and do so by choice, as will be your right.

Nor do you need to worry yourself about the price of heating your home…since you won't require money, which loses its value for you once you cross over…and that which corresponds to our conception of earthly "heat" in the Spirit World is the divine warmth and eternal comfort.

Again, however, in the lower levels reserved for heinous offenders the "climate" is less enticing, and closer in nature to that of the earth plane on a bad day!

One of the major differences you will find between life on earth and your new life in the Spirit World will revolve around something most people take for granted here…*time.*

On earth, we measure all events and situations by what we think of as the passing of time. We have clocks and watches to remind us of how long it will take us to accomplish a given task…when to get up in the morning and retire at night…when to go to work and go home, when to grab our tea break…and have our meals of the day.

Before clocks were invented, humans measured time by the sun and its apparent movements in relation to our own planet. But always…here on the earth plane, we run our lives and regulate everything we do, or intend to do, by time.

Hence the confusion in many people's minds as to how we ever get by without time. But in the Spirit World time ceases to have the relevance it has on earth.

Though spirit people are of course aware of events transpiring on earth, and conscious of birthdays and anniversaries of loved ones still on earth, they do not measure or regulate their lives in the Spirit World in accordance with the concept of time, as we understand time.

For them, according to the many psychics who have received knowledge and information from the higher levels of being, earthly time is illusory…what we think of "the past" being but a fleeting recollection of the mind and the "future" as humans perceive it being simply what we *expect* to happen. It is the eternal "now" that really counts.

We are told by communicating spirits that in the higher realms of the Spirit World past present and future are united in one reality…but these are concepts that really cannot be grasped by a human mind still anchored on the earth plane. All will be revealed, and made comprehensible to us, when we reach that phase of our soul journey.

There is no need to worry about time and how our understanding will change in the afterlife; anymore than you would bother concerning yourself with what the next class at school will be like. When your turn comes, you will adjust to the new circumstances and environment comfortably…as billions of human beings have been doing since the dawn of creation.

Space has a different meaning also in the afterlife. You are not restricted in the way we are down here. You can move to any location you desire to visit with the speed of thought, and see anyone you desire to see or communicate with, provided they have no objection to hearing from you.

As I explained in my previous book, such considerations as what to wear, what to eat, or where to live present no obstacle in the Spirit World. All the great communicators down the centuries confirm that earthly habits relating to food, clothing and living conditions are catered for.

You can eat anything you wish, dress however you fancy, and occupy any dwelling that meets with your approval. There are no supermarkets in the Spirit World that you have to enter with your trolley or shopping basket.

Food is created out of the atmosphere. Everything that exists is energy in one form or another, on earth and in the higher realms, and in the Spirit World you can have anything to eat or drink by asking, or wishing for it.

Houses and other buildings are similarly fashioned from the energies around you, as are the beautiful landscapes and gardens and avenues... the lush vegetation...the gorgeous vistas that stretch before you in alluring charm and a beauty that would dazzle the eyes of a human still enmeshed in his or her mortal body were he or she suddenly transported to that blessed dream come true that is the Spirit World *without preparation.*

So don't despair if you live in relative discomfort or even poverty here on earth. That predicament will be *reversed* once you are free from this mortal existence.

When you cross over, it won't matter if you lived in a hovel and hadn't a shirt on your back or a cent in your purse while struggling down here...You will find yourself in a new, totally transformed situation where happiness and contentment will reign supreme for you.

All your struggles to make ends meet you will have left behind on earth, for in the Spirit World there are no banks, no stock exchanges, no property markets...no financiers or money lenders.

And health-wise, you will have nothing to worry about either. Regardless of what ailment or accident or act of war or human cruelty was responsible for your departure from the earth plane...your spirit remains intact, the REAL YOU is still safe and unharmed.

In the Spirit World, you have perfect health, and no need of a medical card to get the attention of a doctor.

Of course there are hospitals that cater for those humans who have crossed over in especially violent or unnatural circumstances...to enable them to come to terms with the suddenness and traumatic nature of their passing.

And people who have severely abused drugs or alcohol in their earth lives also require special attention, care, and counselling when they reach the Other Side.

Still afraid of death? Reflect on this…what awaits you Over There is not only not to be feared…it will be a vast improvement on your present circumstances, regardless of how fortunate or otherwise you are in your earth incarnation.

This is my promise.

Tiny Tiny Footsteps

Tiny Tiny footsteps,
Tiny whispers too…
Do you know where Heaven is?
Tell me if you do.

Will you come and comfort me?
Will you come and play?
Will you send me feathers
To say you're on your way?

Andrea Bonny

About the Author

Moira Geoghegan is an internationally renowned psychic medium who lives and works in County Kilkenny, Ireland